Lecture Notes in Computer Science 12408

More information about this series at http://www.springer.com/series/7409

Yujiu Yang · Lei Yu · Liang-Jie Zhang (Eds.)

Cognitive Computing – ICCC 2020

4th International Conference
Held as Part of the Services Conference Federation, SCF 2020
Honolulu, HI, USA, September 18–20, 2020
Proceedings

 Springer

Editors
Yujiu Yang
Tsinghua Shenzhen International
Graduate School
Shenzhen, China

Lei Yu
IBM Research – Thomas J. Watson
Research
New York, NY, USA

Liang-Jie Zhang (iD)
Kingdee International Software
Group Co., Ltd,
Shenzhen, China

ISSN 0302-9743   ISSN 1611-3349 (electronic)
Lecture Notes in Computer Science
ISBN 978-3-030-59584-5   ISBN 978-3-030-59585-2 (eBook)
https://doi.org/10.1007/978-3-030-59585-2

LNCS Sublibrary: SL3 – Information Systems and Applications, incl. Internet/Web, and HCI

This Springer imprint is published by the registered company Springer Nature Switzerland AG
The registered company address is: Gewerbestrasse 11, 6330 Cham, Switzerland

Preface

The International Conference on Cognitive Computing (ICCC) was created to cover all aspects of Sensing Intelligence (SI) as a Service (SIaaS). Cognitive Computing is a sensing-driven-computing (SDC) scheme that explores and integrates intelligence from all types of senses in various scenarios and solution contexts. It is well beyond traditional human being's senses, which has four major senses (sight, smell, hearing, and taste) located in specific parts of the body, as well as a sense of touch located all over a body.

ICCC 2020 is a member of the Services Conference Federation (SCF). SCF 2020 had the following 10 collocated service-oriented sister conferences: the International Conference on Web Services (ICWS 2020), the International Conference on Cloud Computing (CLOUD 2020), the International Conference on Services Computing (SCC 2020), the International Congress on Big Data (BigData 2020), the International Conference on AI & Mobile Services (AIMS 2020), the World Congress on Services (SERVICES 2020), the International Congress on Internet of Things (ICIOT 2020), the International conference on Cognitive Computing (ICCC 2020), the International Conference on Edge Computing (EDGE 2020), and the International Conference on Blockchain (ICBC 2020). As the founding member of SCF, the First International Conference on Web Services (ICWS 2003) was held in June 2003 in Las Vegas, USA. Meanwhile, the First International Conference on Web Services - Europe 2003 (ICWS-Europe 2003) was held in Germany in October 2003. ICWS-Europe 2003 was an extended event of ICWS 2003, and held in Europe. In 2004, ICWS-Europe was changed to the European Conference on Web Services (ECOWS), which was held in Erfurt, Germany. To celebrate its 18th birthday, SCF 2020 was held virtually during September 18–20, 2020.

This volume presents the accepted papers of ICCC 2020, held as a fully virtual conference during September 18–20, 2020. The major topics presented at ICCC 2020 included, but were not limited to: Cognitive Computing Technologies and Infrastructure, Cognitive Computing Applications, SI, Cognitive Analysis, Mobile Services, and Cognitive Computing on Smart Home, and Cognitive Computing on Smart City.

We accepted 10 papers, including 8 full papers and 2 short papers. Each was reviewed and selected by three independent members of the ICCC 2020 International Program Committee. We are pleased to thank the authors whose submissions and participation made this conference possible. We also want to express our thanks to the Program Committee members, for their dedication in helping to organize the conference and reviewing the submissions. We thank the volunteers, authors, and conference participants for their great contributions to the fast-growing worldwide services innovations community.

July 2020

Yujiu Yang
Lei Yu
Liang-Jie Zhang

Organization

Program Chairs

Yujiu Yang   Tsinghua Shenzhen International Graduate School,
China
Lei Yu   IBM Thomas J. Watson Research Center, USA

Services Conference Federation (SCF 2020)

General Chairs

Yi Pan   Georgia State University, USA
Samee U. Khan   North Dakota State University, USA
Wu Chou   Vice President of Artificial Intelligence & Software at
Essenlix Corporation, USA
Ali Arsanjani   Amazon Web Services (AWS), USA

Program Chair

Liang-Jie Zhang   Kingdee International Software Group Co., Ltd, China

Industry Track Chair

Siva Kantamneni   Principal/Partner at Deloitte Consulting, USA

CFO

Min Luo   Huawei, USA

Industry Exhibit and International Affairs Chair

Zhixiong Chen   Mercy College, USA

Operations Committee

Jing Zeng   Yundee Intelligence Co., Ltd, China
Yishuang Ning   Tsinghua University, China
Sheng He   Tsinghua University, China
Yang Liu   Tsinghua University, China

Steering Committee

Calton Pu (Co-chair)	Georgia Tech, USA
Liang-Jie Zhang (Co-chair)	Kingdee International Software Group Co., Ltd, China

ICCC 2020 Program Committee

Luca Cagliero	Politecnico di Torino, Italy
Schahram Dustdar	Vienna University of Technology, Austria
Mehmet Emre Gursoy	Georgia Tech, USA
Meng Han	Kennesaw State University, USA
Eleanna Kafeza	Athens University of Economics and Business, Greece
Nagarajan Kandasamy	Drexel University, USA
Supratik Mukhopadhyay	Louisiana State University, USA
Roberto Natella	Federico II University of Naples and Critiware, Italy
Rui André Oliveira	University of Lisbon, Portugal
Stacey Truex	Georgia Tech, USA
Lingling Zhao	Harbin Institute of Technology, China

Conference Sponsor – Services Society

Services Society (S2) is a nonprofit professional organization that has been created to promote worldwide research and technical collaboration in services innovation among academia and industrial professionals. Its members are volunteers from industry and academia with common interests. S2 is registered in the USA as a "501(c) organization," which means that it is an American tax-exempt nonprofit organization. S2 collaborates with other professional organizations to sponsor or co-sponsor conferences and to promote an effective services curriculum in colleges and universities. The S2 initiates and promotes a "Services University" program worldwide to bridge the gap between industrial needs and university instruction.

The services sector accounted for 79.5% of the USA's GDP in 2016. The world's most service-oriented economy, with service sectors accounting for more than 90% of the GDP. S2 has formed 10 Special Interest Groups (SIGs) to support technology and domain specific professional activities:

- Special Interest Group on Web Services (SIG-WS)
- Special Interest Group on Services Computing (SIG-SC)
- Special Interest Group on Services Industry (SIG-SI)
- Special Interest Group on Big Data (SIG-BD)
- Special Interest Group on Cloud Computing (SIG-CLOUD)
- Special Interest Group on Artificial Intelligence (SIG-AI)
- Special Interest Group on Edge Computing (SIG-EC)
- Special Interest Group on Cognitive Computing (SIG-CC)
- Special Interest Group on Blockchain (SIG-BC)
- Special Interest Group on Internet of Things (SIG-IOT)

About the Services Conference Federation (SCF)

As the founding member of the Services Conference Federation (SCF), the First International Conference on Web Services (ICWS 2003) was held in June 2003 in Las Vegas, USA. Meanwhile, the First International Conference on Web Services - Europe 2003 (ICWS-Europe 2003) was held in Germany in October 2003. ICWS-Europe 2003 was an extended event of ICWS 2003, and held in Europe. In 2004, ICWS-Europe was changed to the European Conference on Web Services (ECOWS), which was held in Erfurt, Germany. SCF 2019 was held successfully in San Diego, USA. To celebrate its 18th birthday, SCF 2020 was held virtually during September 18–20, 2020.

In the past 17 years, the ICWS community has expanded from Web engineering innovations to scientific research for the whole services industry. The service delivery platforms have been expanded to mobile platforms, Internet of Things (IoT), cloud computing, and edge computing. The services ecosystem is gradually enabled, value added, and intelligence embedded through enabling technologies such as big data, artificial intelligence (AI), and cognitive computing. In the coming years, all the transactions with multiple parties involved will be transformed to blockchain.

Based on the technology trends and best practices in the field, SCF will continue serving as the conference umbrella's code name for all service-related conferences. SCF 2020 defines the future of New ABCDE (AI, Blockchain, Cloud, Big Data, Everything is connected), which enable IoT and enter the 5G for the Services Era. SCF 2020's 10 collocated theme topic conferences all center around "services," while each focusing on exploring different themes (web-based services, cloud-based services, big data-based services, services innovation lifecycle, AI-driven ubiquitous services, blockchain driven trust service ecosystems, industry-specific services and applications, and emerging service-oriented technologies). SCF includes 10 service-oriented conferences: ICWS, CLOUD, SCC, BigData, AIMS, SERVICES, ICIOT, EDGE, ICCC, and ICBC. The SCF 2020 members are listed as follows:

[1] The International Conference on Web Services (ICWS 2020, http://icws.org/) is the flagship theme-topic conference for Web-based services, featuring Web services modeling, development, publishing, discovery, composition, testing, adaptation, delivery, as well as the latest API standards.

[2] The International Conference on Cloud Computing (CLOUD 2020, http://thecloudcomputing.org/) is the flagship theme-topic conference for modeling, developing, publishing, monitoring, managing, delivering XaaS (Everything as a Service) in the context of various types of cloud environments.

[3] The International Conference on Big Data (BigData 2020, http://bigdatacongress.org/) is the emerging theme-topic conference for the scientific and engineering innovations of big data.

[4] The International Conference on Services Computing (SCC 2020, http://thescc.org/) is the flagship theme-topic conference for services innovation lifecycle that includes enterprise modeling, business consulting, solution creation, services

orchestration, services optimization, services management, services marketing, and business process integration and management.

[5] The International Conference on AI & Mobile Services (AIMS 2020, http://ai1000.org/) is the emerging theme-topic conference for the science and technology of AI, and the development, publication, discovery, orchestration, invocation, testing, delivery, and certification of AI-enabled services and mobile applications.

[6] The World Congress on Services (SERVICES 2020, http://servicescongress.org/) focuses on emerging service-oriented technologies and the industry-specific services and solutions.

[7] The International Conference on Cognitive Computing (ICCC 2020, http://thecognitivecomputing.org/) focuses on the Sensing Intelligence (SI) as a Service (SIaaS) which makes systems listen, speak, see, smell, taste, understand, interact, and walk in the context of scientific research and engineering solutions.

[8] The International Conference on Internet of Things (ICIOT 2020, http://iciot.org/) focuses on the creation of IoT technologies and development of IOT services.

[9] The International Conference on Edge Computing (EDGE 2020, http://theedgecomputing.org/) focuses on the state of the art and practice of edge computing including but not limited to localized resource sharing, connections with the cloud, and 5G devices and applications.

[10] The International Conference on Blockchain (ICBC 2020, http://blockchain1000.org/) concentrates on blockchain-based services and enabling technologies.

Some highlights of SCF 2020 are shown below:

- **Bigger Platform:** The 10 collocated conferences (SCF 2020) are sponsored by the Services Society (S2) which is the world-leading nonprofit organization (501 c(3)) dedicated to serving more than 30,000 worldwide services computing researchers and practitioners. Bigger platform means bigger opportunities to all volunteers, authors, and participants. Meanwhile, Springer sponsors the Best Paper Awards and other professional activities. All the 10 conference proceedings of SCF 2020 have been published by Springer and indexed in ISI Conference Proceedings Citation Index (included in Web of Science), Engineering Index EI (Compendex and Inspec databases), DBLP, Google Scholar, IO-Port, MathSciNet, Scopus, and ZBlMath.
- **Brighter Future:** While celebrating the 2020 version of ICWS, SCF 2020 highlights the Third International Conference on Blockchain (ICBC 2020) to build the fundamental infrastructure for enabling secure and trusted service ecosystems. It will also lead our community members to create their own brighter future.
- **Better Model:** SCF 2020 continues to leverage the invented Conference Blockchain Model (CBM) to innovate the organizing practices for all the 10 theme conferences.

Contents

Research Track

HFF: Hybrid Feature Fusion Model for Click-Through Rate Prediction

Yunzhou Shi and Yujiu Yang$^{(\boxtimes)}$

Tsinghua Shenzhen International Graduate School, Tsinghua University,
Shenzhen, China
syz17@mails.tsinghua.edu.cn, yang.yujiu@sz.tsinghua.edu.cn

Abstract. Deep neural network (DNN) which is applied to extract high-level features plays an important role in the Click Through Rate (CTR) task. Although the necessity of high-level features has been recognized, how to integrate high-level features with low-level features has not been studied well. There are some works fuse low- and high-level features by simply sum or concatenation operations. We argue it is not an effective way because they treat low- and high-level features equally. In this paper, we propose a novel hybrid feature fusion model named HFF. HFF model consists of two different layers: feature interaction layer and feature fusion layer. With feature interaction layer, our model can capture high-level features. And the feature fusion layer can make full use of low- and high-level features. Comprehensive experiments on four real-world datasets are conducted. Extensive experiments show that our model outperforms existing the state-of-the-art models.

1 Introduction

CTR prediction is critical to many web applications including web search, recommendation system, sponsored search, and display advertising. The aim of this task is to estimate the probability that a user clicks on a given item. In online advertising application, which is a billions of dollars scenario, the precision of prediction has a direct impact on the final revenue of business providers. So CTR prediction with high precision is a core task of online advertising.

Combinatorial features are helpful for good performance in CTR prediction task. For example, it is reasonable to recommend *Before Sunrise*, a famous romance movie to an eighteen-year-old girl. In this case, $< Gender = Female, Age = 18, MovieGenre = Romance >$ is a third-order combinatorial feature which is informative for prediction. But it takes great efforts to explore the meaningful combinatorial features, especially when the number of raw features is huge. So a lot of works have been proposed to learn combinatorial features automatically by feature interactions. Factorization Machines (FM) [1–3] and its variants are widely used for modeling pairwise feature interactions.

This work was supported in part by the National Key Research and Development Program of China (No. 2018YFB1601102), and the Shenzhen Science and Technology Project under Grant (GGFW2017040714161462).

It captures second-order combinatorial features by modeling second-order feature interactions. But in real scenario, second-order feature interactions may not have enough expression ability. As aforementioned case, we need third-order feature interactions.

Extensive literatures [3–5] have shown that the high-order feature interactions are crucial for a good performance. With the success of deep learning in computer vision, speech recognition and natural language processing, some works [6–9] have been proposed to utilize DNN for CTR prediction task. They stack multiple interaction layers to extract high-level features. The deeper the network is, the more high-order feature interactions are captured by high-level features. CrossNet [9] applies a multi-layer residual network to learn high-level features. xDeepFM [5] stacks Compressed Interaction Network (CIN), which aims to learn high-order feature interaction explicitly, to extract high-level features. AutoInt cascades [4] multi-head self-attention layers [10] with residual connection for high-level features. But these models achieve the best performance when the depth of DNN is only 3 or 4. The performance of these models drop significantly as the number of interaction layers increases continuously. We argue that when these models go deeper, the high-level features capture more high-order feature interactions and lost more low-order feature interactions which are also essential for prediction. Even the models with residual connection also face the same problem. Although there are some hybrid models which contain low- and high-level features have been studied, such as Wide&Deep [6] and DeepFM [7], they both need extra models to capture low-level features. (Wide&Deep utilizes linear model (wide part) for low-level features. DeepFM applies FM for low-level feature.) What's more, these models fuse high- and low-level features by simple sum or concatenation operations and can't utilize low-level features effectively.

In this paper, we propose a novel hybrid feature fusion model named HFF. HFF model consists of two different layers: feature interaction layer and feature fusion layer. With the feature interaction layer, our model can extract high-level features. The outputs of the first few feature interaction layers can also be utilized as low-level features. So extra part isn't necessary for low-level features in our model. After obtaining high- and low-level features, our feature fusion layer fuses them by multi-head self-attention mechanism. The experimental results show that our feature fusion layer can utilize these low-level features more effectively.

The contribution of our paper are summarized as follows:

- We propose a novel hybrid feature fusion model named HFF for CTR prediction task which can not only extract high-level features but also make full use of low-level features which are also helpful for performance promotion;
- Compared to simple sum or concatenation operations, we adopt multi-head self-attention mechanism to utilize low- and high-level feature effectively;
- We conduct extensive experiments on four real-world dataset, and the results demonstrate that our HFF model outperforms the existing state-of-the-art models.

Our work is organized as follows. In Sect. 2, we summarize the related work. Section 3 presents our proposed model for CTR prediction task. In Sect. 4, we present experimental results and detailed analysis. We conclude this paper in Sect. 5.

2   Related Work

With the rapid development of online advertising, how to predict the probability of a user will click a recommended advertisement plays a significant role in recommendation systems. The accuracy of CTR prediction affects not only user experience but also the revenue of advertising agencies. So CTR prediction task has drawn great attention from both academia and industry.

Combinatorial features are helpful for good performance in CTR prediction task. In order to capture meaningful combinatorial features, engineers have to take a lot of manual efforts for cross features. To tackle the above problem, some models have been proposed to learn combinatorial features automatically by feature interactions. A well-known model is Factorization Machine (FM) [1]. This model transforms features into low dimension latent vector and learns second-order combinatorial features by modeling second-order feature interactions [11,12]. Afterward, different variants of factorization machines have been proposed. Field-aware Factorization Machines (FFM) [2] extends FM by making the feature representation field-specific. AFM [3] improves performance by adding attention net and also offers good explainability.

Although FM based models can learn combinatorial feature automatically, they can only model the second-order feature interactions due to the architecture of FM. With the success of DNN, there are some works have been proposed to modeling higher-order feature interactions by DNN. With the depth of DNN increases, the more high-order feature interactions are captured by high-level features. PNN [13], FNN [14], and DeepCrossing [15] utilized a feed-forward neural network to learn high-level features. CrossNet [9] is proposed to capture high-level features by cross operation AutoInt [4] utilizes multi-head attention mechanism to extract high-level features.

Although DNN models perform well, the fact is that not deeper the DNN is, the better the model performs. With the increasing of network's depth, the low-level features are ignored. This is detrimental to prediction performance. Some hybrid models have been proposed to combine high- and low-level features. Wide&Deep [6] combines a linear model (wide part) for low-level features and a DNN (deep part) for high-level features. In this model, two different inputs are required for the "wide part" and "deep part", respectively, and the input of "wide part" still relies on expertise feature engineering. DeepFM [7] replaces the liner model in Wide&Deep with FM and add the raw features to the output of DNN. Both of the above hybrid models need extra models to capture low-level features and fuse high- and low-level features by simple sum or concatenation operations. To utilize high- and low-level features effectively, we propose a novel hybrid feature fusion model named HFF. The proposed model can capture low- and high-level features and make full use of them. The experimental results on four datasets show the effectiveness of our model.

3   Our Model

In this section, we start with problem definition. For a sample $\{\mathcal{X}, \mathcal{Y}\}$, $\mathcal{X} = \{\mathbf{x}_{field_1}, \cdots, \mathbf{x}_{field_m}, \cdots, \mathbf{x}_{field_M}\}$ is a M-fields features input which records the context information about user and item, and $\mathcal{Y} \in \{0, 1\}$ is the associated label indicating user's click behaviors ($\mathcal{Y} = 1$ means the user clicked the item, and $\mathcal{Y} = 0$ otherwise). $\mathcal{X}$ may include categorical fields (e.g., gender, location) and continuous fields (c.g., age). Each categorical field is represented as a vector of one-hot encoding, and each continuous field is represented as the value itself. Normally, $\mathcal{X}$ is high-dimensional and extremely sparse. The task of CTR prediction is to build a prediction model $\hat{y} = F(\mathcal{X})$ to estimate the probability of a user clicking a specific item in a given context. The overall architecture of our proposed HFF model is shown in Fig. 1. Our model is composed of four parts: Embedding layer, Feature interaction layer, Feature fusion layer and Prediction layer. Compared to existing models, our model not only focuses on modeling high-level features but also make full use of low-level features which are essential to performance.

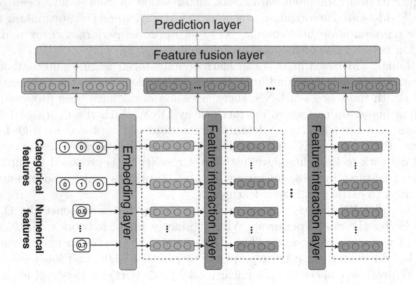

Fig. 1. The overall architecture of our HFF model. Our model is composed of four parts: Embedding layer, Feature interaction layer, Feature Fusion layer and Prediction layer.

3.1   Embedding Layer

For input feature $\mathcal{X} = \{\mathbf{x}_{field_1}, \cdots, \mathbf{x}_{field_m}, \cdots, \mathbf{x}_{field_M}\}$, $\mathbf{x}_{field_m}$ is a one-hot vector if the m-th field is categorical feature, while $\mathbf{x}_{field_m}$ is a scalar value if the m-th field is numerical feature. For categorical feature, it often leads to excessively high-dimensional feature space for large feature size. To reduce such high-dimensional feature space, we employ an embedding procedure (similar to word embedding in NLP) to transform these binary features into dense vectors:

$$\mathbf{e}_m = \mathbf{W}_m \mathbf{x}_{field_m}, \tag{1}$$

where $\mathbf{e}_m \in \mathcal{R}^{d_e}$ is the categorical embedding vector of m-th filed, d_e is the dimension of embedding vector and $\mathbf{x}_{field_m}$ is one-hot input in the m-th field, $\mathbf{W}_m$ is embedding matrix of the m-th field. For the numerical feature, we represent it as:

$$\mathbf{e}_m = \mathbf{w}_m \mathbf{x}_{field_m}, \tag{2}$$

where $\mathbf{w}_m$ is the embedding vector of the m-th field, and $\mathbf{x}_{field_m}$ is the scalar value of the m-th field. Finally, we obtain the input of Intra-layer FI layer as follows:

$$\begin{aligned}\mathbf{H}^0 &= [\mathbf{h}_1^0; \cdots ; \mathbf{h}_m^0; \cdots ; \mathbf{h}_M^0] \\ &= [\mathbf{W}_E \mathbf{e}_1; \cdots ; \mathbf{W}_E \mathbf{e}_m; \cdots ; \mathbf{W}_E \mathbf{e}_M],\end{aligned} \tag{3}$$

where $\mathbf{W}_E \in \mathbb{R}^{d \times d_e}$ is transformation matrix in case of dimension mismatching. d is the number of hidden units of Intra-layer FI layer.

3.2   Feature Interaction Layer

For feature interaction layer, we model high-level features by multi-head self-attention mechanism [10] which was proposed in the area of natural language processing. With this mechanism, it is easy to capture rich and effective feature interactions. The multi-head mechanism transposes features into different semantic subspaces and helps to learn the diversified polysemy of feature. The self-attention mechanism determines which features should be combined to form meaningful high-level features. We stack L feature interaction layers to capture high-level features.

For l-th feature interaction layer, the input is the output of the previous layer $\mathbf{H}^{l-1} = [\mathbf{h}_1^{l-1}; \cdots ; \mathbf{h}_m^{l-1}; \cdots ; \mathbf{h}_M^{l-1}]$. Firstly, we split $\mathbf{h}_m^{l-1}$ into N heads $\{\mathbf{h}_{m,n}^{l-1}\}_{n=1}^N$ and then apply a N heads self-attention setup:

$$\mathbf{h}_m^l = \mathbf{h}_m^{l-1} + [\hat{\mathbf{h}}_{m,1}^l \oplus \cdots \oplus \hat{\mathbf{h}}_{m,n}^l \oplus \cdots \oplus \hat{\mathbf{h}}_{m,N}^l], \tag{4}$$

$$\hat{\mathbf{h}}_{m,n}^l = \sum_{j=1}^M \alpha_{mj,n}^l \mathbf{W}_{V,n}^l \mathbf{h}_{j,n}^{l-1}, \tag{5}$$

$$\alpha_{mj,n}^l = a(\mathbf{h}_{m,n}^{l-1}, \mathbf{h}_{j,n}^{l-1}), \tag{6}$$

where $\oplus$ denotes the concatenation operator and $\mathbf{W}_{V,n}^l \in \mathbb{R}^{d \times d}$ is transformation matrix. Attention function $a(\cdot, \cdot)$ is calculated in the following form:

$$a(\mathbf{q}_m, \mathbf{k}_j) = \frac{exp\left((\mathbf{W}_K \mathbf{k}_j)^T \mathbf{W}_Q \mathbf{q}_m\right)}{\sum_{z=1}^N exp\left((\mathbf{W}_K \mathbf{k}_z)^T \mathbf{W}_Q \mathbf{q}_m\right)}, \tag{7}$$

where $\mathbf{W}_Q, \mathbf{W}_K \in \mathbb{R}^{d \times d}$ are transformation matrices for $\mathbf{q}_m$ and $\mathbf{k}_j$ respectively, and the result is scaled by $\frac{1}{\sqrt{d}}$ [10].

To obtain the output of l-th layer, a norm layer is added:

$$\mathbf{h}_m^l = LayerNorm(ReLU(\hat{\mathbf{h}}_m^l)), \tag{8}$$

where $ReLU(z) = max(0, z)$ is a non-linear activation function.

3.3   Feature Fusion Layer

Previous models focused on modeling high-level features and pay less attention on low-level features which are also essential for prediction accuracy. So we propose feature fusion layer to make full use of low-level features. The input of feature fusion layer is $\mathbf{H} = [\mathbf{h}^0; \cdots; \mathbf{h}^l; \cdots; \mathbf{h}^L]$, which are combined by the outputs of embedding layer and L feature interaction layer. For $\mathbf{h}^l = [\mathbf{h}_1^l \oplus \cdots \oplus \mathbf{h}_m^l \oplus \cdots \oplus \mathbf{h}_M^l]$, $\mathbf{h}^l$ is the output of embedding layer when $l = 0$ and $\mathbf{h}^l$ is the output of l-th feature interaction layer when $l \in \{1, \cdots, L\}$.

For dimension matching, an affine transformation is firstly applied as follows:

$$\begin{aligned} \tilde{\mathbf{H}} &= [\tilde{\mathbf{h}}^0; \cdots; \tilde{\mathbf{h}}^l; \cdots; \tilde{\mathbf{h}}^L] \\ &= [\mathbf{W}_H \mathbf{h}^0; \cdots; \mathbf{W}_H \mathbf{h}^l; \cdots; \mathbf{W}_H \mathbf{h}^L], \end{aligned} \tag{9}$$

where $\mathbf{W}_H \in \mathbb{R}^{d_h \times d}$ is transformation matrix. To utilize all the features effectively, we also adopt muti-head self-attention mechanism to modeling interaction between high-level and low-level features. Firstly, we split $\tilde{\mathbf{h}}^l$ into N heads $\{\tilde{\mathbf{h}}_n^l\}_{n=1}^N$ and then apply a N heads self-attention setup:

$$\hat{\mathbf{o}}^l = \tilde{\mathbf{h}}^l + [\hat{\mathbf{o}}_1^l \oplus \cdots \oplus \hat{\mathbf{o}}_n^l \oplus \cdots \oplus \hat{\mathbf{o}}_N^l], \tag{10}$$

$$\hat{\mathbf{o}}_n^l = \sum_{j=0}^L \alpha_{j,n}^l \mathbf{W}_{V,n}^o \tilde{\mathbf{h}}_{j,n}^{l-1}, \tag{11}$$

$$\alpha_{j,n}^l = a(\tilde{\mathbf{h}}_{m,n}^{l-1}, \tilde{\mathbf{h}}_{j,n}^{l-1}), \tag{12}$$

where $\alpha(\cdot)$ is similar to eq. (7) and $\mathbf{W}_{V,n}^o \in \mathbb{R}^{d_h \times d_h}$ is a transformation matrix. Finally, we obtain the output of feature fusion layer as follows:

$$\mathbf{o}^l = LayerNorm(ReLU(\hat{\mathbf{o}}^l)), \tag{13}$$

3.4   Prediction Layer

We simply concatenate all the output of feature fusion layer and then apply a non-linear projection to predict the click probability:

$$\hat{y} = \sigma(\mathbf{w}^T(\mathbf{o}^0 \oplus \cdots \oplus \mathbf{o}^L) + b), \tag{14}$$

where $\mathbf{w} \in \mathbb{R}^D$ ($D = (L+1) \times d_h$) is a column projection vector, $b \in \mathbb{R}$ is bias, and $\sigma(x) = 1/(1 + \exp(-x))$.

We choose *LogLoss* which is widely used in CTR prediction task as our target loss function:

$$LogLoss = -\frac{1}{N} \sum_{i=1}^{N} \{y_i \log(\hat{y}_i) + (1 - y_i) \log(1 - \hat{y}_i)\}, \tag{15}$$

where y_i and $\hat{y}_i$ are ground truth and predicted user click. N is the total number of training samples. The parameters are learned by minimizing the total *LogLoss* using gradient descent.

4 Experiments

To show the effectiveness of our HFF model, We conduct extensive experiments on four public real-world datasets. We present all the experimental results in this section. Codes for fully reproducibility will be open source soon after necessary polishment.

4.1 Datasets

We evaluate the performance of our model on four public real-world datasets, which are Criteo[1], Avazu[2], KDD12[3] and MovieLens-1M[4]. **Criteo** is a benchmark dataset for CTR prediction published by criteo lab. It contains 26 categorical feature fields and 13 numerical feature fields. **Avazu** contains users' mobile behaviors including whether a displayed mobile ad is clicked by a user or not. It has 23 feature fields spanning from user/device features to ad attributes. **KDD12** was released by KDDCup 2012, which originally aimed to predict the number of clicks. Since our work focuses on CTR prediction rather than the exact number of clicks, we treat this problem as a binary classification problem (1 for clicks, 0 for without click). **MovieLens-1M** contains users'ratings on movies. During binarization, we treat samples with a rating less than 3 as negative samples because a low score indicates that the user does not like the movie. We treat samples with a rating greater than 3 as positive samples and remove neutral samples, i.e., a rating equal to 3. In Table 1, we present the statistics of the four datasets.

4.2 Data Preparation

All the data preparation strategies are similar to AutoInt [4]. First, we remove the infrequent features (appearing in less than threshold instances), where threshold is set to 10, 5, 10 for Criteo, Avazu and KDD12 data sets respectively. And we keep all features for MovieLens-1M. Then, we normalize numerical values by

---

[1] https://www.kaggle.com/c/criteo-display-ad-challenge.
[2] https://www.kaggle.com/c/avazu-ctr-prediction.
[3] https://www.kaggle.com/c/kddcup2012-track2.
[4] https://grouplens.org/datasets/movielens/.

Table 1. Statistics of experimental dataset.

Data	#Samples	#Fields
Criteo	45,840,617	39
Avazu	40,428,967	23
KDD12	149,639,105	13
MovieLens-1M	730,012	7

Table 2. Performance of CTR prediction on four datasets.

Model	Criteo		Avazu		KDD12		MovieLens-1M	
	AUC	Logloss	AUC	Logloss	AUC	Logloss	AUC	Logloss
LR	0.7820	0.4695	0.7560	0.3964	0.7631	0.1684	0.7716	0.4424
FM [1]	0.7836	0.4700	0.7706	0.3856	0.7759	0.1573	0.8252	0.3998
Wide&Deep [6]	0.8026	0.4494	0.7749	0.3824	0.7549	0.1619	0.8300	0.3976
Deep&Cross [9]	0.8067	0.4447	0.7731	0.3836	0.7869	0.1549	0.8446	0.3809
AFM [3]	0.7938	0.4584	0.7718	0.3854	0.7659	0.1591	0.8227	0.4048
NFM [8]	0.7957	0.4562	0.7708	0.3864	0.7515	0.1631	0.8357	0.3883
DeepFM [7]	0.8066	0.4449	0.7751	0.3829	0.7867	0.1549	0.8437	0.3846
xDeepFM [5]	0.8070	0.4447	0.7770	0.3823	0.7820	0.1560	0.8463	0.3808
AutoInt [4]	0.8061	0.4454	0.7752	0.3823	0.7883	0.1546	0.8460	0.3784
HFF (ours)	**0.8073**	**0.4441**	**0.7754**	**0.3822**	**0.7890**	**0.1542**	**0.8486**	**0.3744**

transforming a value z to $log^2(z)$ if $z > 2$. Finally, we randomly select 80% of all samples for training and randomly split the rest into validation and test sets with equal size.

Evaluation Metrics. We use two metrics to evaluate the performance of all models: **AUC** (Area Under the ROC curve) and **Logloss** (cross entropy).

– **AUC.** AUC measures the probability that a positive instance will be ranked higher than a randomly chosen negative one. It only takes into account the order of predicted instances and is insensitive to class imbalance problem. A higher AUC indicates a better performance.
– **Logloss.** Logloss measures the distance between the predicted score and the true label for each instance. This metric is defined in Eq. 15.

It is noticeable that a slightly higher AUC or lower Logloss at **0.001**-level is regarded significant for CTR prediction task, which has also been pointed out in existing works [6,7,9].

Model Comparison. We compare 9 models in our experiments: LR, FM [1], Wide&Deep [6], Deep&Cross [9], AFM [3], NFM [8], DeepFM [7], xDeepFM [5], and AutoInt [4].

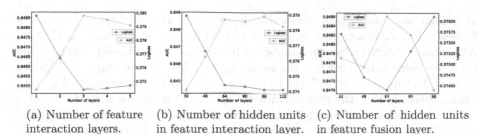

(a) Number of feature interaction layers.   (b) Number of hidden units in feature interaction layer.   (c) Number of hidden units in feature fusion layer.

Fig. 2. Impact of network hyper-parameters on AUC and Logloss performance.

Implementation Details. Our models are trained to minimize the loss in Eq. 15 in an end-to-end fashion. We choose Adam as optimizer. The embedding size is 16 and the number of attention head is 2. The number of hidden units for feature interaction layer and feature fusion layer are both 64. We set the number of feature interaction layers to 3.

4.3 Experimental Results

The performance for CTR prediction of different models on four datasets is shown in Table 2. In CTR prediction tasks, a slightly higher AUC or Logloss value at 0.001-level is regarded as a huge improvement. We can observe that our HFF model outperforms all other models on four datasets. This shows the effectiveness of our HFF model. Note that AutoInt also utilizes the same multi-head self-attention mechanism as our HFF model to capture high-level feature. But AutoInt performs worse than our model on four datasets. Our model also outperforms hybrid models like Wide&Deep and DeepFM. All the above observations indicates the importance of feature interaction layer and the effectiveness of our feature fusion layer.

4.4 Analysis

The Efffect of Hyper-Parameters. In this section, we mainly analysis the impact of hyper-parameters on our HFF model. We conduct experiments on MovieLens-1M dataset and analysis from the following three aspects: the number of feature interaction layers, the number of hidden units in feature interaction layer and the number of hidden units in feature fusion layer.

As shown in Fig. 2(a), model performance increases steadily when increasing the number of feature interaction layers from 1 to 3 and achieves best performance when the layer number is 3. However, when the number of feature interaction layers is greater than 3, the model performance degrades. So the most suitable number of feature interaction layers is 3.

Figure 2(b) and 2(c) demonstrate how the number of hidden units in feature interaction layer and feature fusion layer impact the model performance. In Fig. 2(b), our model achieves the best performance on Logloss when the number of hidden units in feature interaction layer is 64. But our model obtain the highest AUC value when the number of hidden units is 80. Considering that the AUC value achieved when the number of hidden units is 64 is only slightly lower than the value achieved when the number is 80. We set the number of hidden units in feature intercation layer to 64 for less model parameters. In Fig. 2(c), we can observe that the performance of our model increases with the number of hidden units in feature fusion layer. However, model performance degrades when the number of hidden units in feature fusion layer is set greater than 64.

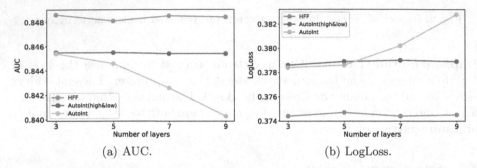

(a) AUC.   (b) LogLoss.

Fig. 3. Performance w.r.t the number of interaction layers for different models.

Analysis on Effectiveness and Efficiency. To prove the effectiveness of our HFF model, we conduct the following experiments on MovieLens-1M dataset.

We choose AutoInt [4] as our comparative model because it extracts high-level feature with the same multi-head self-attention mechanism as our HFF model. And we also keep the number of hidden units in interaction layer equally for AutoInt and our HFF model. If the number of feature interaction layers is L, AutoInt only utlizes the features of the last L-th interaction layer to predict the result and ignores the low-level features captured by the first 1-th to $(L-1)$-th interaction layers. To prove the importance of low-level features, We add a model named AutoInt(high&low). The AutoInt(high&low) concatenates the outputs of all L interaction layers in AutoInt to predict the result.

As shown in Fig. 3, with the increase of interaction layers, the performance of AutoInt degrades quickly because the information in low-level features lost. But AutoInt(high&low) and our HFF model don't perform badly as the number of interaction layers increases, which exactly shows the importance of low-level features. Our HFF model still outperforms AutoInt(high&low) which introduces low-level features by simple concatenation operation. It demonstrates the power of our feature fusion layer.

We fix the number of feature interaction layers to 3 and decrease the number of hidden units for feature interaction layer and feature fusion layer from 64 to 40. As shown in Tab. 3, our HFF model has less parameters than AutoInt. But our little model still performs better than AutoInt, which furtherly demonstrates the efficiency and the effectiveness of our model.

Table 3. Efficiency comparison between AutoInt and HFF.

Model	#Params	AUC	Logloss
AutoInt	3.9×10^4	0.8460	0.3784
HFF	$\mathbf{3.2 \times 10^4}$	**0.8462**	**0.3767**

5 Conclusion

In this paper, we proposed a novel model named HFF for CTR prediction. HFF consists of feature interaction layer and feature fusion interaction. So, our model can not only capture high-level feature, but also make full use of low-level feature whichs most high-level based models ignore. The experimental results on four open datasets show the effectiveness of our approach.

References

1. Rendle, S.: Factorization machines. In: ICDM 2010, pp. 995–1000 (2010)
2. Juan, Y., Zhuang, Y., Chin, W., Lin, C.: Field-aware factorization machines for CTR prediction. In: RecSys 2016, pp. 43–50 (2016)
3. Xiao, J., Ye, H., He, X., Zhang, H., Wu, F., Chua, T.: Attentional factorization machines: learning the weight of feature interactions via attention networks. In: IJCAI 2017, pp. 3119–3125 (2017)
4. Song, W., et al.: Autoint: automatic feature interaction learning via self-attentive neural networks. In: Proceedings of the 28th ACM International Conference on Information and Knowledge Management, CIKM 2019, Beijing, China, 3–7 November, pp. 1161–1170 (2019)
5. Lian, J., Zhou, X., Zhang, F., Chen, Z., Xie, X., Sun, G.: xDeepfm: combining explicit and implicit feature interactions for recommender systems. In: ACM SIGKDD 2018, pp. 1754–1763 (2018)
6. Cheng, H., et al.: Wide & deep learning for recommender systems. In: DLRS@RecSys 2016, pp. 7–10 (2016)
7. Guo, H., Tang, R., Ye, Y., Li, Z., He, X.: Deepfm: a factorization-machine based neural network for CTR prediction. In: IJCAI 2017, pp. 1725–1731 (2017)
8. He, X., Chua, T.: Neural factorization machines for sparse predictive analytics. In: ACM SIGIR 2017, pp. 355–364 (2017)
9. Wang, R., Fu, B., Fu, G., Wang, M.: Deep & cross network for ad click predictions. In: ADKDD 2017, pp. 1–7 (2017)
10. Vaswani, A., et al.: Attention is all you need. In: NIPS 2017, pp. 6000–6010 (2017)
11. Rendle, S., Freudenthaler, C., Schmidt-Thieme, L.: Factorizing personalized Markov chains for next-basket recommendation. In: WWW 2010, pp. 811–820 (2010)
12. Rendle, S., Gantner, Z., Freudenthaler, C., Schmidt-Thieme, L.: Fast context-aware recommendations with factorization machines. In: ACM SIGIR 2011, pp. 635–644 (2011)
13. Qu, Y., et al.: Product-based neural networks for user response prediction. In: ICDM 2016, pp. 1149–1154 (2016)

14. Zhang, W., Du, T., Wang, Jun: Deep learning over multi-field categorical data. In: Ferro, N., et al. (eds.) ECIR 2016. LNCS, vol. 9626, pp. 45–57. Springer, Cham (2016). https://doi.org/10.1007/978-3-319-30671-1_4
15. Shan, Y., Hoens, T.R., Jiao, J., Wang, H., Yu, D., Mao, J.C.: Deep crossing: Web-scale modeling without manually crafted combinatorial features. In: ACM SIGKDD 2016, pp. 255–262 (2016)

PRTransE: Emphasize More Important Facts Based on Pagerank for Knowledge Graph Completion

Zhongwen Li[1], Bin Zhang[1,2], Yang Liu[1,2], and Qing Liao[1,2(✉)]

[1] Harbin Institute of Technology (Shenzhen), Shenzhen 518055, China
calmerzwl@gmail.com, bin.zhang@pcl.ac.in, {liu.yang,liaoqing}@hit.edu.cn
[2] Peng Cheng Laboratory, Shenzhen, China

Abstract. Knowledge graph is a hot research field in the direction of artificial intelligence. The task of knowledge graph completion is to predict the links between entities. Translation-based models (such as TransE, TransH, and TransR) are a class of well-known knowledge graph completion methods. However, most existing translation-based models ignore the importance of triplets in the completion process. In this paper, we propose a novel knowledge graph completion model PRTransE, which considers the importance information of triplets based on PageRank and combines the importance information of triplets with knowledge graph embedding. Specifically, PRTransE integrates the entity importance and relationship importance of the triplet at the same time, and adopts different processing methods for the importance information of the positive and negative tuples, so that the proposed method pays adaptive attention to different triplet information in the learning process and improve learning performance to achieve better completion effect. Experimental results show that, in two real-world knowledge graph datasets, PRTransE has the best overall performance in terms of link prediction task compared to the five comparison models.

Keywords: Knowledge graph · Entity importance · Relation importance · Link prediction

1 Introduction

Knowledge graphs such as WordNet [1], Freebase [2] and Yago [3] have become important resources in many AI applications, such as web/mobile search, question answering(Q&A), etc. They usually contain extensive structured data as the form of triplets $(head\_entity, relation, tail\_entity)$(denoted as (h, r, t)), where relation represents the relationship between the two entities. Although a typical knowledge graph may contain a great many triplets that represent numerous facts, they usually suffer from incompleteness. Knowledge graph completion aims at predicting relations between entities based on existing triplets in a knowledge

© Springer Nature Switzerland AG 2020
Y. Yang et al. (Eds.): ICCC 2020, LNCS 12408, pp. 15–26, 2020.
https://doi.org/10.1007/978-3-030-59585-2_2

graph. In the past decade, much work based on formal logic has been done for knowledge graph completion [4–7], but they are neither tractable nor robust for a real large scale knowledge graph.

Recently, a promising approach for this task is to encode a knowledge graph into a low-dimensional embedding vector space. Following this approach, many methods have been explored, which will be introduced in detail in Sect. 2. Among these methods, TransE [8,9] is simple and effective, achieving the state-of-the-art prediction performance. It learns vector embeddings for both entities and relationships. These vector embeddings are denoted by the same letter in boldface. The basic idea behind TransE is that, every relation is regarded as translation between the embeddings of entities, that is, $\mathbf{h} + \mathbf{r} \approx \mathbf{t}$ when (h, r, t) holds. TransE is suitable for 1-to-1 relations, but has issues when dealing with N-to-1,1-to-N and N-to-N relations. TransH [10] is proposed to address these flaws, it enables an entity having different representations when involved in different relations by utilizing relation-specific hyperplane, which is denoted by a norm vector $\mathbf{w}_r$ and a translation vector $\mathbf{d}_r$. The embedding vectors $\mathbf{h}$ and $\mathbf{t}$ are projected to the hyperplane of relation r to obtain vectors $\mathbf{h}_{\perp} = \mathbf{h} - \mathbf{w}_r^T \mathbf{h} \mathbf{w}_r$ and $\mathbf{t}_{\perp} = \mathbf{t} - \mathbf{w}_r^T \mathbf{h} \mathbf{w}_r$, then $\mathbf{h}_{\perp} + \mathbf{d}_r \approx \mathbf{t}_{\perp}$. The common assumption is entities and relations are in the same vectore space for TransE and TransH. However, entities and relations are different types of objects, they should be in different vector space. TransR [11] projected $\mathbf{h}$ and $\mathbf{t}$ to the aspects that relation r focuses on through the mapping matrix $\mathbf{M}_r$ and then $\mathbf{M}_r \mathbf{h} + \mathbf{r} \approx \mathbf{M}_r \mathbf{t}$.

However, those methods all do not consider the importance information of different triplets. It is intuitive that different facts or different entities have different importance level, some triplets are more important than other triplets. Hence, during learning the information in knowledge graph, we should pay different attention to different triplets. To address this issue, we propose a new approach **PRTransE**, which considers importance information in learning knowledge graph triplets and obtain importance by PageRank mainly, hence named as PRTransE. Our contributions in the paper are as follows:

- We propose a novel model PRTransE, which consider importance information into knowledge graph completion. It provides a flexible approach to deal with different triplets in a knowledge graph.
- Compared with TransE, PRTransE pays different attention to various triplets during learning knowledge graph facts.
- In experiments, our approach outperforms previous methods including TransE, TransH, TransR in link prediction task.

2   Related Work

We first define our notations. (h, r, t) denotes a triplet and bold lower case **h,r,t** denotes their column vectors; bold upper case letters denotes matrices, such as $\mathbf{M}$. $f_r(\mathbf{h}, \mathbf{t})$ represents score funtion. The score is expected to be lower for a golden triplet and higher for an incorrect triplet. Other notations will be described in the appropriate sections.

2.1   Translation-Based Models

As mentioned in Section "Introduction", TransE regards the relation $\mathbf{r}$ as the translation from $\mathbf{h}$ to $\mathbf{t}$ for a golden triplet, i.e. the pair of embedded entities in a triplet (h, r, t) could be linked by $\mathbf{r}$ with slight error if (h, r, t) is a golden triplet. This indicates that $(\mathbf{t})$ should be a nearest neighbor of $(\mathbf{h} + \mathbf{r})$, while $(\mathbf{h} + \mathbf{r})$ should be far away from $\mathbf{t}$ otherwise. The score function is

$$f_r(\mathbf{h}, \mathbf{t}) = \|\mathbf{h} + \mathbf{r} - \mathbf{t}\|_2^2 \tag{1}$$

TransE is suitable for 1-to-1 relations, but has issues for N-to-1,1-to-N and N-to-N relations. To solve these problems, TransH enabled an entity to have different representations on hyperplanes of different relations. For a relation r, TransH models the relation as a relation-specific translation vector $\mathbf{r}$ on a relation-specific hyperplane with $\mathbf{w}_r$ as the normal vector rather than in the same space of entity embeddings. Concretely, for a triplet (h, r, t), the entity embedding $\mathbf{h}$ and $\mathbf{t}$ are first projected to the hyperplane $\mathbf{w}_r$. The projecting vectors are denoted as $\mathbf{h}_\perp$ and $\mathbf{t}_\perp$, respectively. The score function is defined as

$$f_r(\mathbf{h}, \mathbf{t}) = \|\mathbf{h}_\perp + \mathbf{r} - \mathbf{t}_\perp\|_2^2 \tag{2}$$

TransH ensures that $\mathbf{h}_\perp$ and $\mathbf{t}_\perp$ are on the hyperplane of r by restricting $\|\mathbf{w}_r\| = 1$. The common assumption is entities and relations are in the same vectore space for TransE and TransH. Although TransH extxtends modeling flexibility by emploiting relation hyperplanes, it does not perfectly break the restriction of this assumption. However, entities and relations are different types of objects, they should be in different vector space.

Hence, TransR is proposed based on the assumption, which models entities and relations in distinct spaces, i.e. entity space and relation space. TransR uses a relation-specific projection matrix $\mathbf{M}_r$ for each r to map entities into a relation specific subspace. The score function of TransR is:

$$f_r(\mathbf{h}, \mathbf{t}) = \|\mathbf{M}_r \mathbf{h}_\perp + \mathbf{r} - \mathbf{M}_r \mathbf{t}_\perp\|_2^2 \tag{3}$$

2.2   Other Models

In addition to translation-based models, semantic matching models utilize similarity-based scoring functions. They measure the credibility of facts by matching the underlying semantics of the entities and the relationships contained in the vector space representation.

In DISTMULT [12], entities are represented by vectors, and relationships are represented by diagonal matrices, which model pairwise interactions between potential factors, and the scoring function is a bilinear function.

ComplEx [13] extended DISTMULT model to better model the asymmetric relationship by introducing complex number. Then, the entities and relationships are in the complex space, and the fact of asymmetric relationship can get different scores according to the order of the involved entities.

3   Model

To take into account the importance of different triplets, we purpose PRTransE, which introduces the triplet importance in a natural way mainly based on pagerank.

3.1   PRTransE

The triplet importance includes two parts: 1) entity importance. 2) relation importance. In addition, the knowledge graph datasets include positive triplets and negative triplets. And the PRTransE adopts respective process for positive triplets and negative triplets. The model PRTransE is shown in Fig. 1.

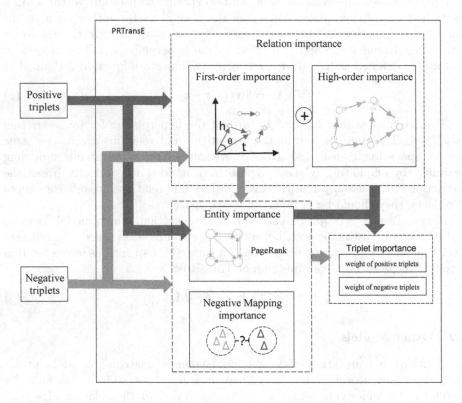

Fig. 1. The model structure of PRTransE

3.2   Entity Importance

For entity importance [14] in positive triplets and negative triplets, the PageRank is used to compute it. The idea of PageRank is originally used to measure the importance of webpage on the Internet. And different nodes have different importances on the web network. Inspired by L Page et al. [15], the idea of PageRank is used to compute entity importance in knowledge graph. For entity importance in negative triplets, it adopts the similar PageRank algorithm as in positive triplets.

$$E_{imp}(h_i) = \frac{1-d}{N} + d \sum_{h_j \in M(h_i)} \frac{E_{imp}(h_j)}{L(h_j)} \tag{4}$$

where h_i represents the entity which is to be estimated the importance, $M(h_i)$ is the set of entities that link to h_i, N is total number of entities in the knowledge graph, d is damping coefficient, $L(h_j)$ represents the number of outlinks of the entity h_j.

3.3   Relation Importance

For relation importance in positive triplets, the model had an assumption that the importance of a relation is not only affected by first order relation [16] but also by higher order relation. For the estimation of relation importance in first order relation, PRTransE adopts the Jaccard similarity of relations.

$$R_{imp_1}(r_i) = \frac{h_i \cdot t_i}{||h_i||_2 ||t_i||_2} \tag{5}$$

where R_{imp_1} represents the first-order importance of relation r_i in the triplet (h_i, r_i, t_i). h_i and t_i are embedding vectors represent head entity and tail entity respectively. $||.||_2$ is the module of corresponding vector.

For the higher order importance of the relationship, the model regards the association of the head entity, tail entity and the relationship in the triplet as "voting" for the relationship, and then combines the entity importance to obtain the higher order importance of the relationship. For example, as shown in Fig. 2, assume that r is a 3–2 relationship, but for the formation of the triplet (h2, r, t2), the head entity's association with the relationship can be regarded as a "vote". Similarly, the same is true for tail entity. Divide the importance scores of the entities at both ends by the number of alternative paths, and then combine to obtain the higher-order importance of the relationship in the triplet.

The following is a formula for calculating the higher-order importance of a relationship:

$$R_{imp_2}(r_i) = \frac{E_{imp}(h_i)}{h_{r_i} p t_{r_i}} + \frac{E_{imp}(t_i)}{t_{r_i} p h_{r_i}} \tag{6}$$

where $R_{imp_2}(r_i)$ means higher-order importance of relation r_i, $E_{imp}(h_i)$ and $E_{imp}(t_i)$ represents importance score of entity h_i and t_i respectively, $h_{r_i} p t_{r_i} = \frac{\#(\Delta_{r_i})}{\#distinct(t_{r_i})}$ [17], where t_{r_i} represents the tail entities belonging to relationship r_i, and Δ_{r_i} denotes the training triplets containing the relationship r_i. $h_{r_i} p t_{r_i}$ represents the average number of triplets corresponding to each tail entity in the

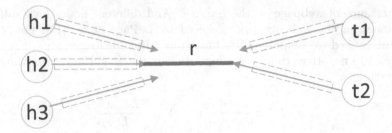

Fig. 2. The diagram of higher-order importance of relation

relationship r_i Similarly, $t_{r_i}ph_{r_i} = \frac{\#(\Delta_{r_i})}{\#distinct(h_{r_i})}$, $t_{r_i}ph_{r_i}$ represents the average number of triplets corresponding to each head entity in the relationship r_i.

Hence, the relation importance affected by higher order relation is obtained. Then, the comprehensive relation importance score $R_{imp}(r_i)$ could be gained by combinating first order importance with higher order importance. Here, there is calculation formula:

$$R_{imp}(r_i) = \alpha * R_{imp_1}(r_i) + (1 - \alpha) * R_{imp_2}(r_i) \tag{7}$$

where α is a hyperparameter, used to weigh the first-order importance and higher-order importance of the relationship.

In the above manner, we obtained the first-order importance score and the higher-order importance score of the relationship, and combined the two to obtain the overall relationship importance score.

3.4   Triplet Importance

After obtaining entity importance and relationship importance, for the i-th positive triplet $ptri_i$, such as (h_i, r_i, t_i), the importance score $w_+(ptri_i)$ of the positive triplet can be calculated. The formula is defined as follows:

$$w_+(ptri_i) = \frac{E_{imp}(h_i) + E_{imp}(t_i) + R_{imp}(r_i)}{3} \tag{8}$$

However, for relation importance in negative triplets, there exists some difference compared to situations in the positive triplets: 1) Negative triplets are generated by replacing the correct entities in the positive triplets with other entities, and the replaced entities will in most cases cause the original triplets to be invalid, resulting in incorrect matching of information. Since the information in the knowledge graph flows through the entire network through relationships, mismatched entities can cause incorrect information to flow, thus destroying the higher-order importance of the relationship. Therefore, for negative triplets, the model does not consider the higher order importance of the relationship. 2) Since the model learns negative samples during training, it can improve the model's ability to recognize wrong tuples when making link predictions. Therefore, the model considers the importance of negative triplet mapping importance W_{r_i}, and its purpose is to strengthen the learning process of negative triplets, this factor is obtained by combining $h_{r_i}pt_{r_i}$ and $t_{r_i}ph_{r_i}$. The formula is as follows:

$$W_{r_i} = \frac{1}{log(h_{r_i}pt_{r_i} + t_{r_i}ph_{r_i})} \tag{9}$$

where W_{r_i} is a weight coefficient arising from $h_{r_i}pt_{r_i}$ and $t_{r_i}ph_{r_i}$.
Hence, for the i-th negative triplet $ntri_i$ e.g. (h_i, r_i, t'_i), its importance score $w_-(ntri_i)$ is

$$w_-(ntri_i) = \frac{E_{imp}(h_i) + E_{imp}(t'_i) + R_{imp_1}(r_i) + W_{r_i}}{4} \tag{10}$$

where $E_{imp}(h_i)$ and $E_{imp}(t'_i)$ are the importance score of entity h_i and t'_i, $R_{imp_1}(r_i)$ represents the first-order importance of relation as Eq.(7), W_{r_i} represents the mapping importance of the relationship in the negative triplet.

Algorithm 1 Learning PRTransE

Input: Training set $S = \{(h, r, t)\}$ and $S' = \{(h', r, t')\}$, entity and relation sets E and L, margin γ, S' is produced from S by some replacement strategy.
1: Initialize $pt \leftarrow$ for each triplet $s \in S$
2:     $nt \leftarrow$ for each triplet $s' \in S'$
3: **loop**
4:   **for** $(h_i, r_k, t_j) \in S$ $(resp., (h_i, r_k, t'_j) \in S')$ **do**
5:     $E_{imp}(h_i) \leftarrow \frac{1-d}{N} + d \sum\limits_{h_j \in M(h_i)} \frac{E_{imp}(h_j)}{L(h_j)}$
6:     $R_{imp_1}(r_i) \leftarrow \frac{h_i \cdot t_i}{||h_i||_2 ||t_i||_2}$
7:     $R_{imp_2}(r_i) \leftarrow \frac{E_{imp}(h_i)}{h_{r_i}pt_{r_i}} \mid \frac{E_{imp}(t_i)}{t_{r_i}ph_{r_i}}$
8:     $R_{imp}(r_i) \leftarrow \alpha * R_{imp_1}(r_i) + (1 - \alpha) * R_{imp_2}(r_i)$
9:     $w_+(ptri_i) \leftarrow \frac{E_{imp}(h_i) + E_{imp}(t_i) + R_{imp}(r_i)}{3}$
10:    $W_{r_i} \leftarrow \frac{1}{log(h_{r_i}pt_{r_i} + t_{r_i}ph_{r_i})}$
11:    $(resp. w_-(ntri_i) \leftarrow \frac{E_{imp}(h_i) + E_{imp}(t'_i) + R_{imp_1}(r_i) + W_{r_i}}{4})$
12: **end for**
13: Update embeddings w.r.t.
   $\sum_{(h,r,t) \in S} \sum_{(h',r,t') \in S'} \nabla[\gamma + w_+(ptri_i)d(h + r, t) - w_-(ntri_i)d(h' + r, t')]_+$
14: **end loop**

---

4   Experiments and Analysis

4.1   Datasets and Evaluation Protocol

To evaluate our proposed method, we use two benchmark datasets. They are from two popular knowledge graphs: WordNet(Miller 1995) and Freebase(Bollacker et al. 2008). WordNet is a large lexical knowledge graph. Entities in Word-Net are synonyms which represent distinct concepts. Relations in WordNet are conceptual-semantic and lexical relations. Freebase is a large collaborative knowledge base consists of a great many the world facts, such as triplets (Peter Finch, location, london) and (Yoshinaga_Sayuri, profession, actor). Table 1 lists statistics of the 2 dataset.

Table 1. The summary of datasets

Datasets	#Relation	#Entity	#Train samples	#Valid samples	#Test samples
WN18	18	40,943	141,442	5,000	5,000
FB15k	1,345	14,951	483,142	50,000	59,071

The purpose of the link predicion task is to predict a triplet (e_i, r_k, e_j) which lacks e_i or e_j, i.e. predict e_i given (r_i, e_j) or predict e_j given (e_i, r_k). The task emphasizes the rank of the correct entity instead of only finding the best one entity. Similarly to (Bordes et al. 2013), we exploit two metrics as our ecaluation protocols: the average rank of all correct entities(Mean Rank) and the proportion of correct entities ranked in top N ranks(Hits@N) for N = 1, 3, and 10. A lower Mean Rank and a higher Hits@N mean the performance of model is better.

4.2   Experiment Setup

We first describe the notations We assume that there are n_t triplets in the training set, $(h_i, r_i, t_i)(i = 1, 2, ..., n_t)$ denotes the i-th triplets. Each triplet has a label y_i indicating that the triplet is positive($y_i = 1$) or negative($y_i = 0$). Then the positive triplet set $S = \{(h_j, r_j, t_j)|y_j = 1\}$, the negative triplet set $S' = \{(h_j, r_j, t_j)|y_j = 0\}$. However, the knowledge graph originally contains only positive training triplets, not negative training triplets. Therefore, we obtain a positive triplet set S from the knowledge graph, and then generate a negative triplet set according to the generating rules: $S' = \{(h_l, r_k, t_k)|h_l \neq h_k \wedge y_k = 1\} \cup \{(h_k, r_k, t_l)|t_l \neq t_k \wedge y_k = 1\}$, that is to replace the head entity or tail entity in a positive triplet with a wrong entity to generate a negative triplet. In addition, according to previous research work, there are two commonly used methods for replacement strategies: "Unif" and "Bern". "Unif" refers to randomly replacing the head entity or tail entity for a positive triplet, but the knowledge graph itself is pretty incomplete. This random sampling method may introduce many wrong negative triplets for training. The "Bern" strategy takes more into account the mapping properties of the relationships in the triplets, and then has different probabilities for replacing the head entity or tail entity. For example, the mapping properties of relationships in the knowledge graph are divided into 1−1, 1−N, N−1 and N−N. If a relation is 1−N, the "Bern" strategy tends to replace the head entity with a large probability. If the relation is N-to-1, it tends to replace the tail entity with a large probability.

Here, We define the following margin-based training object function

$$L = \sum_{(h,l,t)\in S} \sum_{(h',l,t')\in S'} [\gamma + w_+(ptri_i)d(h+r,t) - w_-(ntri_i)d(h'+r,l')]_+ \quad (11)$$

where $[x]_+$ represents the positive part of x, $\gamma > 0$ is a margin hyperparameter, S is the set of positive triplets and S' is the set of negative triplets. $d(h+r,t)$ represents the distance score(or energy score) of a triplet. For example, for a positive triplet $(h,r,t), h+r \approx t$, so its distance score $d(h+r,t)$ should be small, and for a negative triplet, its distance score is larger, the $L1$ norm or $L2$ norm can be used to calculate the distance. The process of minimizing the objective function can be performed using stochastic gradient descent.

In this task, we use two datasets: FB15 K and WN18. We select the margin γ among $\{1, 1.5, 2, 2.5, 3\}$, the dimension of entity vectors m and the dimension of relation vectors n among $\{50, 100, 150\}$, and the mini-batch size B among $\{100, 500, 1000\}$. The best configuration obtained by valid set are: $\gamma = 1, m, n = 50, B = 200$ and taking L_2 as dissimilarity. For all the datasets. We traverse to training for 2000 rounds.

4.3 Link Prediction

The task of link prediction is to predict the missing h or t for a golden triplet (h, r, t). In the task, we remove the head/tail entity and then replace it with all the entities in the knowledge graph. For each position of missing entity, the model is asked to rank a set of candidate entities from the knowledge graph, instead of finding the best one result. We first achieve scores of those corrupted triplets and then rank them by descending order, the rank of the correct entity is finally stored. Noting the fact that a corrupted triplet may also exist in knowledge graphs, the corrupted triplet should be regard as a correct triplet. Hence, we should remove the corrupted triplets included in train set, valid set and test set before ranking. Hence, there are two evaluation setting: "Raw"(the corrupted triplets are not removed) and "Filter"((the corrupted triplets are removed).The paper will report evaluation results of the two settings.

Experimental results on all the datasets are shown in Table 2. From Table 2, we can conclude that: (1) PRTransE outperforms other baseline embedding models(TransE, TransH, TransR). (2) On both FB15 K and WN18 public datasets, PRTransE has achieved a consistent improvement in Mean Rank. It suggests that considering triplet importance will benefit knowledge graph completion. (3) On FB15K, PRTransE's HITS@10 performance under the "Raw" setting is slightly weaker than ComplEx, but the HITS@10 performance under the "Filter" setting is better than all comparative models; On the WN18 public dataset, PRTransE's Mean Rank and HITS@10 indicators performed better than the comparison model, indicating that when PRTransE performs entity link prediction, the location of the correct candidate entity is predicted to be more advanced and more accurate.

Table 2. Average results of link prediction

Model	FB15 K				WN18			
	Mean Rank		HITS@10/%		Mean Rank		HITS@10/%	
	Raw	Filter	Raw	Filter	Raw	Filter	Raw	Filter
TransE	243	125	34.9	47.1	263	251	75.4	89.2
TransH	212	87	45.7	64.4	318	303	75.4	86.7
TransR	198	77	48.2	68.7	238	225	79.8	92
ComplEx	275.6	173.4	**50.4**	67.3	306	291	79.0	89.4
DistMult	264.9	167.7	47.3	61.2	250.3	235.9	76.4	87.3
PRTransE	**189.6**	**54.1**	49.2	**72.0**	**232.8**	**220.4**	**80.5**	**92.7**

On the FB15 K data set, under the "Raw" setting, the Mean Rank indicator of PRTransE is improved by about 21.9% compared to the TransE model, and the HITS@10 indicator is improved by about 41.0% compared to TransE; Under the "Filter" setting, the Mean Rank indicator of PRTransE is improved by about 56.7% compared to TransE, and the HITS@10 indicator is improved by 52.9% compared to TransE.

On the WN18 data set, PRTransE has a consistent improvement on all indicators compared to the comparison model. Under the "Raw" setting, the Mean Rank indicator of PRTransE is improved by approximately 11.5% compared to TransE, and the HITS@10 indicator is improved by about 6.8% compared to TransE; Under the "Filter" setting, the Mean Rank indicator of PRTransE is improved by about 12.2% compared to TransE, and the HITS@10 indicator is improved by about 3.9% compared to TransE.

The TransE model and other comparison models do not consider the importance information of the triplet, thus the validity of the PRTransE model in considering the triplet importance information in knowledge graph completion is verified.

5   Conclusion

In this paper, we proposed a knowledge graph completion model based on PageRank and triplet importance, and combines the triplet importance information in the knowledge graph on the basis of TransE, which is used to take appropriate degree of attention for different triplets during model learning, improving the prediction ability of the model. In addition, when considering the importance information of triplets, the importance information hidden in the knowledge graph is fully explored, which makes the model more reasonable when evaluating the importance of triplets during the training process and improves the performance of the model. Experimental result shows that compared with TransE and other knowledge representation models, PRTransE has achieved the best overall performance, and has achieved consistent performance improvements on almost all kinds of indicators.

Acknowledgement. This work is partly supported by National Key Research and Development Program of China (2017YFB0802204) and National Natural Science Foundation of China (No.U1711261).

References

1. Miller, G.A.: Wordnet: a lexical database for english. Commun. ACM **38**(11), 39–41 (1995)
2. Bollacker, K., Evans, C., Paritosh, P., Sturge, T., Taylor, J.: Freebase: a collaboratively created graph database for structuring human knowledge. In: Proceedings of the 2008 ACM SIGMOD International Conference on Management of Data, pp. 1247–1250 (2008)
3. Fabian, M., Gjergji, K., Gerhard, W., et al.: Yago: a core of semantic knowledge unifying wordnet and wikipedia. In: 16th International World Wide Web Conference, WWW, pp. 697–706 (2007)
4. Socher, R., Chen, D., Manning, C.D., Ng, A.: Reasoning with neural tensor networks for knowledge base completion. In: Advances in Neural Information Processing Systems, pp. 926–934 (2013)
5. Dettmers, T., Minervini, P., Stenetorp, P., Riedel, S.: Convolutional 2D knowledge graph embeddings. In: Thirty-Second AAAI Conference on Artificial Intelligence (2018)
6. Zhu, Y., Liu, H., Wu, Z., Song, Y., Zhang, T.: Representation learning with ordered relation paths for knowledge graph completion. arXiv preprint arXiv:1909.11864 (2019)
7. Kazemi, S.M., Poole, D.: Simple embedding for link prediction in knowledge graphs. In: Advances in Neural Information Processing Systems, pp. 4284–4295 (2018)
8. Bordes, A., Usunier, N., Garcia-Duran, A., Weston, J., Yakhnenko, O.: Translating embeddings for modeling multi-relational data. In: Advances in Neural Information Processing Systems, pp. 2787–2795 (2013)
9. Han, X., et al.: Openke: an open toolkit for knowledge embedding. In: Proceedings of the 2018 Conference on Empirical Methods in Natural Language Processing: System Demonstrations, pp. 139–144 (2018)
10. Wang, Z., Zhang, J., Feng, J., Chen, Z.: Knowledge graph embedding by translating on hyperplanes. Aaai. **14**, pp. 1112–1119 (2014)
11. Lin, Y., Liu, Z., Sun, M., Liu, Y., Zhu, X.: Learning entity and relation embeddings for knowledge graph completion. In: Twenty-Ninth AAAI Conference on Artificial Intelligence (2015)
12. Yang, B., Yih, W.T., He, X., Gao, J., Deng, L.: Embedding entities and relations for learning and inference in knowledge bases. arXiv preprint arXiv:1412.6575 (2014)
13. Trouillon, T., Welbl, J., Riedel, S., Gaussier, É., Bouchard, G.: Complex embeddings for simple link prediction (2016)
14. Park, N., Kan, A., Dong, X.L., Zhao, T., Faloutsos, C.: Estimating node importance in knowledge graphs using graph neural networks. In: Proceedings of the 25th ACM SIGKDD International Conference on Knowledge Discovery & Data Mining, pp. 596–606 (2019)
15. Page, L., Brin, S., Motwani, R., Winograd, T.: The pagerank citation ranking: bringing order to the web. Technical report, Stanford InfoLab (1999)

16. Wang, C.C., Cheng, P.J.: Translating representations of knowledge graphs with neighbors. In: The 41st International ACM SIGIR Conference on Research & Development in Information Retrieval, pp. 917–920 (2018)
17. Fan, M., Zhou, Q., Chang, E., Zheng, F.: Transition-based knowledge graph embedding with relational mapping properties. In: Proceedings of the 28th Pacific Asia Conference on Language, Information and Computing, pp. 328–33 (2014)

Context Based Quantum Language Model with Application to Question Answering

Qin Zhao[1], Chenguang Hou[2], and Ruifeng Xu[1(✉)]

[1] Harbin Institute of Technology, Shenzhen 518055, China
xuruifeng@hit.edu.cn
[2] Centre for Remote Imaging, Sensing and Processing, National University of Singapore, 10 Lower Kent Ridge Road, Blk S17, Level 2, Singapore 119076, Singapore

Abstract. Equipped with quantum probability theory, quantum language models (QLMs) aimed at a principled approach to modeling term dependency have drawn increasing attention. However, even though they are theoretically more general and have effective performance, current QLMs do not take context information into account. The most important element, namely density matrix, is constructed as a summation of word projectors, whose representation is independent of context information. To address this problem, we propose a Context based Quantum Language Model (C-QLM). Between word embedding and sentence density matrix, a bidirectional long short term memory network is adopted to learn the hidden context information. Then a set of vectors is utilized to extract density matrices's features for question and answer sentences which can be used to calculate the matching score. Experiment results on TREC-QA and WIKI-QA datasets demonstrate the effectiveness of our proposed model.

Keywords: Context information · Quantum language model · Question answering

1 Introduction

Language Models (LM) have become more and more important in Artificial Intelligence related areas, such as Information Retrieval (IR) and Natural Language Processing (NLP) tasks. Statistical language models and neural language models are two types of the commonly used LMs [1,2]. Statistical language models based on classical probability theory to compute a joint probability distribution over a sequence of a words [3,4], have been intensively studied. Recently, as a generalization of the classical probability theory [5,6], quantum probability theory based quantum-inspired language models have also drawn increasing attention [7,8].

Sordoni, Nie and Bengio proposed a Quantum Language Model (QLM) applied in Information Retrieval (IR) task [7]. Inspired by quantum probability

© Springer Nature Switzerland AG 2020
Y. Yang et al. (Eds.): ICCC 2020, LNCS 12408, pp. 27–38, 2020.
https://doi.org/10.1007/978-3-030-59585-2_3

theory, they aimed to model the term dependency in a more principled way. In this model, the probability uncertainties of words and word compounds are encoded via quantum density matrix, whose off-diagonal terms can measure the interactions between different terms. The ranking of documents for a query is according to the von-Neumann divergence between the density matrices of the query and every document. Applied to ad-hoc information retrieval task, QLM has achieved effective performance.

In order to further develop the capacity of quantum language models, Zhang et al. proposed a Neural Network based Quantum-like Language Model (NNQLM) [9], which is an end-to-end trainable network. Word embedding vectors are viewed as quantum state vectors, based on which sentence-level density matrix can be constructed. Then a joint representation of question and answer sentences is derived via a direct multiplication of their density matrices. A Convolutional Neural Network (CNN) is adopted to extract useful features from this joint representation and shows a great improvement over QLM.

Recently, Li et al. [10] built a Complex valued Network for Matching (CNM) with application in question answering. with well-defined mathematical constrains and explicit physical meaning, all linguistic units are unified in a single complex-valued vector space. Each word is encoded as a complex-valued vector, with vector's length being the relative weight of the word and the phase representing a superposition. Experiment results show the effectiveness of CNM.

Despite the progress in quantum-inspired language models, there is still a limitation. In most quantum language models, sentence representation is derived from word representation. That is, first encode each word with word embedding and construct the corresponding word projector, then treat sentence as a combination of a series of words and build sentence representation via operation similar to a summation of word projectors. In this case, different word representations in the same sentence are independent to each other. However, for general natural language processing tasks, it is well-known that context information plays an important role in word's representation. So it is reasonable to construct word representation equipped with its context information.

In this paper, we propose a Context based Quantum Language Model (C-QLM), where context information is learned via a Bidirectional Long Short Term Memory (BiLSTM) network. Then the output of the BiLSTM layer is adopted to construct sentence density matrix. We utilise a set of measurement vectors to extract features from question and answer density matrices. The proposed C-QLM is applied to a typical Question Answering (QA) task, namely Answer Selection, which aims to find most appropriate answer from candidate answers for a question. Two commonly used QA datasets are used to measure the model's performance, namely TREC-QA and WIKI-QA. Experiment results show that our proposed model equipped with context information is practically well-performed.

2   Related Work

Quantum theory is one of the most important discoveries in the world and has been applied to quite a few areas. For example, it has been applied in social science and economics [11]. The emerging research field of cognition shows that there are quantum-like phenomena in human cognition, especially in language understanding [12–16]. In this section, we briefly introduce the related work in quantum inspired work in Information Retrieval (IR) and Question Answering (QA) tasks.

In Information Retrieval (IR), van Rijsbergen (2004) for the first time proposed to utilize the mathematical formalism of quantum theory to the logical, geometric, and probabilistic IR models [17]. After this pioneering work, a number of quantum-inspired work has been done [18,19,21] based on the analogy between quantum phenomena and natural language processing tasks. Zuccon et al. proposed a quantum probability ranking principle by considering the inter-document dependency as a kind of quantum interference phenomena [19]. A filtering process in photon polarization also has been utilized to construct a quantum-inspired ranking method [20].

Recently, Sordoni, Nie and Bengio [7] came up with a Quantum Language Model (QLM), which is a generalization of the traditional language model. The quantum probability theory is adopted to describe the uncertainty of single and compound terms. Later, Sordoni et al. proposed a supervised way to learn latent concept embeddings for query expansion [22]. To describe the dynamic information need in search session, Li et al. [23] built an adaptive QLM with an evolution process of the density matrix.

Later, the quantum language models has been developed in QA tasks. Zhang et al. [9] proposed an end-to-end Neural Network based Quantum-like Language Model and showed a good performance on QA tasks. Based on complex Hilbert space and projection theory, Li et al. [10] came up with a Complex-valued Network for Matching and achieved comparable performances to strong CNN and RNN baselines.

In this paper, we aim to tackle the problem in general quantum language models, namely the lack of context information in construction of sentence density matrix. In the following section, we show the detailed construction of our proposed model.

3   Basic Concepts

In quantum probability theory [24,25], the probabilistic space is naturally encapsulated in a vector space, specifically a Hilbert space, noted as $\mathbb{H}^n$. We adopt Dirac's notation to denote a unit vector in this space. A unit vector $\vec{u} \in \mathbb{H}$ and its transpose $\vec{u}^T$ are respectively written as a *ket* $|u\rangle$ and a *bra* $\langle u|$. $\langle u|v\rangle$ represents the inner product between two state vectors $|u\rangle$ and $|v\rangle$. The projector onto the direction $|u\rangle$, written as $|u\rangle\langle u|$, is an outer product of $|u\rangle$ itself. Each rank-one projector $|u\rangle\langle u|$ is an elementary event of the quantum probability space, also called a *dyad*. After choosing an orthonormal basis $\{|e_i\rangle\}_{i=1}^n$ for $\mathbb{H}^n$, we can expand an arbitrary vector $|u\rangle$ along each base:

$$|u\rangle = \sum_{i=1}^n u_i |e_i\rangle. \tag{1}$$

where u_i is the probability amplitude along $|e_i\rangle$ and satisfies $\sum_i u_i^2 = 1$.

A density matrix ρ is a symmetric, positive semi-definite matrix with trace being one. It is a generalization of the conventional finite probability distributions in quantum theory, by considering a mixture over dyads,

$$\rho = \sum_i p_i |\psi_i\rangle\langle\psi_i|, \tag{2}$$

where $\{|\psi_i\rangle\}_{i=1}^n$ are pure states and $p_i \geq 0$ is the corresponding probability. This decomposition always exists for density matrices. By Gleason's theorem [26,27], a density matrix is the unique way of defining quantum probability measures, according to

$$\mu_\rho(|u\rangle\langle u|) = \mathrm{tr}(\rho|u\rangle\langle u|). \tag{3}$$

tr is a trace operator. This measure μ ensures that $\mu(|u\rangle\langle u|\rho) \geq 0$.

4 Context Based Quantum Language Model

In quantum language model, the semantic space is treated as a Hilbert space $\mathbb{H}^n$, spanned by a set of orthogonal basis states $\{|e_j\rangle\}_{j=1}^n$, with $|e_j\rangle$ being a sememe representing a semantic unit [28]. Under this background, our proposed Context based Quantum Language Model (C-QLM) is constructed, as shown in Fig. 1. It consists of several parts: a word encoder, sentence density matrix, density matrix feature selector, and feature matching between question and answer sentences. Detailed components of C-QLM is presented as follows.

4.1 Word Encoder

A word w is treated as a superposition of sememes $\{|e_j\rangle\}_{j=1}^n$, with the value vector along sememes encoded with its word embedding. Such a representation of each word can viewed as an observed state in the quantum system. To obtain a unit state vector, we utilize a L2 normalization to restrict every word w to a unit length as follows:

$$|w\rangle = \frac{\vec{w}}{\|\vec{w}\|}, \tag{4}$$

where $\|\vec{w}\|$ denotes L2-norm of $\vec{w}$.

In normal quantum language model, a word projector is constructed based on word state vector, and consequently sentence density matrix is built. In this situation, words are individually independent. However, it is well-known that context can play a significant role in word's representation. Therefore, in order

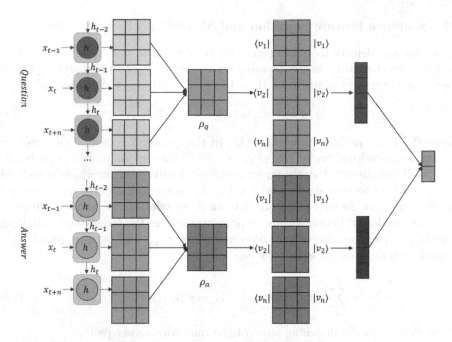

Fig. 1. Context based Quantum Language Model (C-QLM).

to consider context effects, a BiLSTM network is equipped after word encoding. Given a sentence $\{w_t\}_{t=1}^n$, we can obtain:

$$\overrightarrow{h_t} = \overrightarrow{LSTM}(w_t), t \in [1, n]. \tag{5}$$

$$\overleftarrow{h_t} = \overleftarrow{LSTM}(w_t), t \in [1, n]. \tag{6}$$

$$h_{output} = \text{Concat}[\overrightarrow{h_t}, \overleftarrow{h_t}]. \tag{7}$$

Here, $\overrightarrow{h_t}$ denotes the output of the forward-directional LSTM, and $\overleftarrow{h_t}$ denotes the output of the opposite-directional LSTM. Concatenating $\overrightarrow{h_t}$ and $\overleftarrow{h_t}$ gives us the Therefore, each hidden state contains the information from context.

4.2 Sentence Density Matrix with Hidden Projector

A sentence can be represented as a mixed state represented by a density matrix. According to the definition of density matrix, we can create it as

$$\rho_s = \sum_i^n p_i |h_i\rangle\langle h_i|, h_i \in \{h_{output}\}, \tag{8}$$

where $|h_i\rangle\langle h_i|$ is the outer product, and p_i is the probability of each hidden state and satisfy $\sum_i p_i = 1$. It can be seen that this density matrix is context based, due to the contribution of hidden states. It is more powerful than the original density matrix which is a simple summation of word projectors.

4.3   Sentence Feature Selection and Matching

After sentence density matrix is constructed, a series of trainable states can be used to extract density matrix features via measuring state's probability. Given a set of measurement states $\{|\lambda_k\rangle\}_{k=1}^{K}$, the probability for each state $|\lambda_k\rangle$ is

$$|\lambda_k\rangle : P_{\lambda_k} = \langle\lambda_k|\rho_s|\lambda_k\rangle, k \in [1, K], \tag{9}$$

where P_{λ_k} is the probability of state $|\lambda_k\rangle$ in the quantum system. Therefore, we obtain K dimensional vector $[P_{\lambda_1}, P_{\lambda_2}, \cdots, P_{\lambda_K}]$ corresponding to the probabilities of all measurement states under sentence density matrix, which is treated as the sentence feature representation. Do the same operation to question and answer sentences, so we can obtain feature representations for both sentences. A cosine similarity between those representations is treated as the matching score of the question-answer pairs, denoted as $Score_{qa}$. The back propagation is trained with negative cross entropy loss:

$$\mathcal{L} = -\sum_{i}^{N}[y_i\log(Score_{qa}) + (1 - y_i)\log(1 - Score_{qa})], \tag{10}$$

where $Score_{qa}$ is the matching score of the question-answer pairs.

5   Experiment

5.1   Datasets and Evaluation Metrics

Experiments are conducted on two standard benchmarking question answering datasets, namely

- TREC-QA [29]: a standard QA dataset in the Text REtrieval Conference (TREC).
- WIKI-QA [30]: an open domain QA dataset released by Microsoft Research.

On both datasets, the task aims to select the most appropriate answer from the candidate answers for a question. Data cleaning process is operated to remove the questions with no correct answers and the statistics of the cleaned datasets are shown in Table 1. The two commonly used evaluation metrics for the same task with the same datasets, namely mean average precision (MAP) and mean reciprocal ranking (MRR), are used to measure the performance of models.

5.2   Baselines

A wide range comparison with standard quantum inspired models and typical neural networks is made. First, since C-QLM is a quantum inspired model, we compare its performance with those of other closed quantum inspired models. They are

Table 1. Statistics of TREC-QA and WIKI-QA datasets.

Dataset	Question			Pairs		
	Train	Dev	Test	Train	Dev	Test
TREC-QA	1229	65	68	53417	117	1442
WIKI-QA	837	126	633	8627	1130	2351

- **QLM** [7]. Density matrices ρ_q and ρ_a for question and answer sentences are diagonal matrices, with diagonal elements being term frequency values of the corresponding words. von-Neumann divergence between ρ_q and ρ_a is used to measure the matching score of question-answer pairs.
- **NNQLM-II** [9]. It is an end-to-end language model. Based on word embedding, density matrix representing a sentence can encode a mixture of semantic information. Joint representation of question-answer density matrices is used to compute the matching score.
- **CNM** [10]. Words are encoded with complex-valued embedding. A local context segment is used to construct local mixture density matrix and sentence representation. Projectors is trained to select density matrix's features. Than a cosine similarity between the features of density matrices of question and answer sentences features is calculated to measure the matching score.

Besides, in order to compare our proposed model with basic neural networks, we also include basic and typical CNN-based and LSTM-based QA models. On TREC-QA, they include Ngram-CNN [31,32], Multi-Perspective CNN (MP-CNN) [33] and three-layer stacked bidirectional Long Short-term Memory with BM25 (Three-Layer BiLSTM with BM25) [34]. On WIKI-QA, they include Ngram-CNN [31,32] and Long Short-term Memory with attention (LSTM-attn) [35].

5.3 Implementation Details

For C-QLM, the hyper parameters are the word embedding values for each word w, LSTM hidden states, and the projector vectors $\{|\lambda_k\rangle\}_{k=1}^{K}$ used to measure density matrix's features. The word embeddings are initialized with 50-dimension Glove vectors and updated during training. We adopt the Adam optimizer with learning rate amid [1e−4, 5e−4, 1e−3]. Batch size is chosen between [16, 32, 64].

5.4 Experimental Results

Table 2 shows the experiment results on TREC-QA and WIKI-QA datasets, where bold values are the best performances. Our models outperforms other models on most measurements on TREC-QA and WIKI-QA datasets. This demonstrates the effectiveness of our proposed model. The detailed comparison between the results of our model and those of other models is presented as follows:

Table 2. Results on TREC-QA and WIKIQA. The best performed values are in bold.

Model	TREC-QA		WIKIQA	
	MAP	MRR	MAP	MRR
Ngram-CNN	0.6709	0.7280	0.6661	0.6851
MP-CNN	0.7770	0.8360	/	/
Three-Layer BiLSTM with BM25	0.7134	0.7913	/	/
LSTM-attn	/	/	0.6639	0.6828
QLM	0.6784	0.7265	0.5109	0.5148
NNQLM-II	0.7589	0.8254	0.6496	0.6594
CNM	0.7701	0.8591	**0.6748**	0.6864
C-QLM	**0.7834**	**0.8657**	0.6691	**0.6912**

First, on TREC-QA dataset, compared with quantum language model, C-QLM significantly surpass QLM by a rate of 15.48% on MAP and 19.16% on MRR respectively, outperforms NNQLM-II by 3.23% on MAP and 4.88% on MRR respectively, and exceed CNM by a rate of 1.73% on MAP and 0.76% on MRR respectively. Compared with standard and basic CNN and RNN, C-QLM also has an outstanding performance: dramatically outperforms Ngram-CNN by 16.77% on MAP and 18.91% on MRR, respectively; performs better than MP-CNN by 8.24% on MAP and 3.55% on MRR, and surpass Three-Layer BLSTM with BM25 by 9.81% on MAP and 9.40% on MRR.

Second, on WIKI-QA dataset, C-QLM also significantly performs better than QLM by a rate of 30.96% on MAP and 34.27% on MRR, exceed NNQLM-II by 3.00% on MAP and 4.82%, and has a comparable performance with CNM and standard CNN/RNN models.

The experiment results demonstrate the computational effectiveness of C-QLM. The density matrix in QLM and NNQLM-II is built upon direct summation of word projectors, which lacks of context information. Local density scheme in CNM can encode parts of the context information. LSTM in C-QLM encoding context information can improve density matrix's representation.

6 Discussion

We conduct a detailed ablation analysis to investigate the influence of each component on our proposed model. The ablation studies are divided into two groups to investigate the respective effects of context information, and the density matrix. Experiment results are shown in Table (3) and explained as detailed below:

Ablation Study on Context Information. One of the novelty of this paper is to construct a context based sentence density matrix. To achieve this property,

Table 3. Ablation analysis.

Model	TREC-QA		WIKIQA	
	MAP	MRR	MAP	MRR
C-QLM-no-LSTM	0.7597	0.8297	0.6149	0.6251
C-QLM-uni-LSTM	0.7641	0.8504	0.6601	0.6804
C-QLM-class	0.7365	0.8107	0.6329	0.6515
C-QLM	0.7834	0.8657	0.6691	0.6912

a bidirectional LSTM is piped after word embedding. Here, we examine the detailed contribution of this context information via removing the LSTM layer. In this case, two models are built, namely C-QLM-no-LSTM and C-QLM-single-LSTM. C-QLM-no-LSTM is a model without LSTM layer, and C-QLM-uni-LSTM is a model equipped with a unidirectional LSTM layer. On TREC-QA dataset, Table (3) shows that C-QLM-no-LSTM is lower than C-QLM by 3.05% on MAP and 4.16% on MRR respectively. On WIKI-QA dataset, C-QLM-no-LSTM is significantly lower than C-QLM by 8.10% on MAP and 9.56% on MRR respectively. The performance of C-QLM-uni-LSTM is much loser to that of C-QLM. This proves the context information plays an important role to improve model's performance. A unidirectional LSTM can also learn quit a lot context information, and a bidirectional LSTM can be even better.

Ablation Study on Density Matrix. Remember that quantum language model's main property is to use density matrix describing sentence representation. Density matrix entails the information of sememes interactions which can not be revealed in classical neural networks. In this part, we do ablation study on density matrix to directly see how this quantum interaction contribute to the model's performance. C-QLM-class is a model with density matrix layer being replaced by a full connection layer. Table (3) shows that without sememes's interaction, on TREC-QA dataset, C-QLM-class is significantly lower than C-QLM by 6.00% on MAP and 9.36% on MRR respectively. On WIKI-QA dataset, C-QLM-class is lower than C-QLM by a rate of 5.41% on MAP and 5.74% on MRR respectively. It is noted that the number of variables in density matrix is equal to the number of diagonal terms. From the experiment result, we can conclude that the off-diagonal terms which characterize the sememes's interaction without introduce more variable contribute much to the performance of the model.

C-QLM has not yet outperformed CMN on all measurements. On WIKI-QA dataset, C-QLM's performance is quite close to that of CMN. In surpass CMN on MRR, but is lower than that on MAP. The result The possible reason is that although LSTM can learn useful context information for sentence representation, the max length of answer sentences in WIKI-QA dataset is much longer than that in TREC-QA dataset. Concretely, in WIKI-QA dataset, the max length is 214, but in TREC-QA dataset, that is only 42. LSTM may not be able to learn enough context information when a sentence is too long. To overcome this problem, it would be useful to deeper LSTM structure. For example, an answer in WIKI-QA usually contains several sentences. In order to keep long term information, hierarchy LSTM structure could be potential choice. Based on hierarchy structure, a more powerful density matrix could be constructed. In the future, we will systematically analyze and evaluate this mechanisms.

7 Conclusion

In this paper, we propose a Context based Quantum Language Model (C-QLM), where context information is learned via a Bidirectional Long Short Term Memory (BiLSTM) network. Based on the output of BiLSTM network, sentence density matrix naturally contains context information. We apply our model to a typical Question Answering (QA) task, namely Answer Selection, which aims to find most appropriate answer from candidate answers for a question. Experiment results on TREC-QA and WIKI-QA datasets demonstrate the effectiveness of our proposed C-QLM. Our model surpasses most quantum inspired language models, and also performs better than typical CNN and LSTM baselines. In conclusion, our model equipped BiLSTM can learn context information and construct more powerful density matrix, which lead to our model's practically well performance.

Acknowledgments. This work was partially supported by National Natural Science Foundation of China 61632011, 61876053, Shenzhen Foundational Research Funding JCYJ2018 0507183527919, Key Technologies Research and Development Program of Shenzhen JSGG20170817140856618, Guangdong Province Covid-19 Pandemic Control Research Funding 2020KZDZX1224, China Postdoctoral Science Foundation 2020M670912.

References

1. Bengio, Y., Ducharme, R., Vincent, P., Janvin, C.: A neural probabilistic language model. J. Mach. Learn. Res. **3**, 1137–1155 (2003)
2. Mikolov, T., Sutskever, I., Chen, K., Corrado, G.S., Dean, J.: Distributed representations of words and phrases and their compositionality. In: Proceeding of Neural Information Processing Systems, pp. 3111–3119 (2013)
3. Manning, C.D., Raghavan, P., Schutze, H.: Introduction to Information Retrieval. Cambridge University Press, New York (2008)
4. Zhai, C.: Statistical Language Models For Information Retrieval. Synthesis Lectures on Human Language Technologies. Morgan & Claypool Publishers, San Rafael (2008)
5. Melucci, M.: Quantum mechanics and information retrieval. In: Melucci, M., Baeza-Yates, R. (eds.) Introduction to Information Retrieval and Quantum Mechanics. TIRS, vol. 35, pp. 101–188. Springer, Heidelberg (2015). https://doi.org/10.1007/978-3-662-48313-8_3
6. Sordoni, A., Nie, J.-Y.: Looking at vector space and language models for IR using density matrices. In: Atmanspacher, H., Haven, E., Kitto, K., Raine, D. (eds.) QI 2013. LNCS, vol. 8369, pp. 147–159. Springer, Heidelberg (2014). https://doi.org/10.1007/978-3-642-54943-4_13

7. Sordoni, A., Nie, J., Bengio, Y.: Modeling term dependencies with quantum language models for IR. In: Proceeding of Special Interest Group on Information Retrieval, pp. 653–662. ACM (2013)
8. Levine, Y., Yakira, D., Cohen, N., Shashua, A.: Deep learning and quantum entanglement: fundamental connections with implications to network design. arXiv preprint arXiv:1704.01552 (2017)
9. Zhang, P., Niu, J., Su, Z., Wang, B., Ma, L., Song, D.: End-to-end quantum-like language models with application to question answering. In: Proceeding of Association for the Advancement of Artificial Intelligence, pp. 5666–5673 (2018)
10. Li, Q., Wang, B., Melucci, M.: CNM: an interpretable complex-valued network for matching. In: Proceeding of North American Chapter of the Association for Computational Linguistics, pp. 4139–4148 (2019)
11. Haven, E., Khrennikov, A.: Quantum Social Science. Cambridge University Press, Cambridge (2013)
12. Fisher, M.P.A.: Quantum cognition: the possibility of processing with nuclear spins in the brain. Ann. Phys. **362**, 593–602 (2015)
13. Bruz, P., Wang, Z., Busemeyer, J.: Quantum cognition: a new theoretical approach to psychology. Trends Cogn. Sci. **19**(7), 383–393 (2015)
14. Busemeye, J.R., Bruza, P.: Quantum Models of Cognition and Decision. Cambridge University Press, Cambridge (2012)
15. Zhang, P., Song, D., Hou, Y., et al.: Automata modeling for cognitive interference in users relevance judgment. In: Proceedings of the AAAI-Fall 33th Symposium on Quantum Informatics for Cognitive, Social and Semantic Processes, pp. 125–133 (2010)
16. Basile, I., Tamburini, F.: Towards quantum language models. In: Proceedings of the 2017 Conference on Empirical Methods in Natural Language Processing, pp. 1840–1849 (2017)
17. van Rijsbergen, C.J.: The Geometry of Information Retrieval. Cambridge University Press, Cambridge (2004)
18. Piwowarski, B., Frommholz, I., Lalmas, M., van Rijsbergen, K.: What can quantum theory bring to information retrieval. In: Proceeding of Conference on Information and Knowledge Management, pp. 59–68 (2010)
19. Zuccon, G., Azzopardi, L.: Using the quantum probability ranking principle to rank interdependent documents. In: Gurrin, C., et al. (eds.) ECIR 2010. LNCS, vol. 5993, pp. 357–369. Springer, Heidelberg (2010). https://doi.org/10.1007/978-3-642-12275-0_32
20. Zhao, X., Zhang, P., Song, D., Hou, Y.: A novel re-ranking approach inspired by quantum measurement. In: Clough, P., et al. (eds.) ECIR 2011. LNCS, vol. 6611, pp. 721–724. Springer, Heidelberg (2011). https://doi.org/10.1007/978-3-642-20161-5_79
21. Zhang, P., et al.: A quantum query expansion approach for session search. Entropy **18**(4), 146 (2016)
22. Sordoni, A., Bengio, Y., Nie, J.: Learning concept embeddings for query expansion by quantum entropy minimization. In: Proceeding of Association for the Advancement of Artificial Intelligence, vol. 14, pp. 1586–1592 (2014)
23. Li, Q., Li, J., Zhang, P., Song, D.: Modeling multi-query retrieval tasks using density matrix transformation. In: Proceeding of Special Interest Group on Information Retrieval, pp. 871–874. ACM (2015)
24. Neumann, V.: Mathematical Foundations of Quantum Mechanics, vol. 2. Princeton University Press, Princeton (1955)

25. Nielsen, M.A., Chuang, I.L.: Quantum Computation and Quantum Information. Cambridge University Press, Cambridge (2010)
26. Gleason, A.M.: Measures on the closed subspaces of a Hilbert space. J. Appl. Math. Mech. **6**(6), 885–893 (1957)
27. Hughes, R.I.: The Structure and Interpretation of Quantum Mechanics. Harvard University Press, Cambridge (1992)
28. Goddard, C., Wierzbicka, A.: Semantic and Lexical Universals: Theory and Empirical Findings. John Benjamins Publishing, Amsterdam (1994)
29. Voorhees, E.M., Tice, D.M.: Building a question answering test collection. In: Proceeding of Special Interest Group on Information Retrieval, pp. 200–207 (2000)
30. Yang, Y., Yih, W., Meek, C.: WikiQA: a challenge dataset for open-domain question answering. In: Proceeding of Empirical Methods in Natural Language Processing, pp. 2013–2018. ACL (2015)
31. Severyn, A., Moschitti, A.: Learning to rank short text pairs with convolutional deep neural networks. In: Proceeding of Special Interest Group on Information Retrieval, pp. 373–382. ACM (2015)
32. Severyn, A., Moschitti, A.: Modeling relational information in question-answer pairs with convolutional neural networks. arXiv preprint arXiv:1604.01178 (2016)
33. He, H., Gimpel, K., Lin, J.: Multiperspective sentence similarity modeling with convolutional neural networks. In: Proceeding of Empirical Methods in Natural Language Processing, pp. 1576–1586. ACL (2015)
34. Wang, D., Nyberg, E.: A long short-term memory model for answer sentence selection in question answering. In: Proceeding of Association for Computational Linguistics, pp. 707–712 (2015)
35. Miao, Y., Yu, L., Blunsom, P.: Neural variational inference for text processing. arXiv preprint arXiv:1511.06038 (2015)

Improving Fake Product Detection with Aspect-Based Sentiment Analysis

Jiaming Li, Yonghao Fu, Daoxing Liu, and Ruifeng Xu(✉)

Harbin Institute of Technology (Shenzhen), Shenzhen 518055, China
lijm_hitsz@163.com, 18340852925@163.com, daoxingliu@163.com,
xuruifeng@hit.edu.cn

Abstract. With the development of e-commerce, the number of counterfeit products is increasing and the rights and interests of customers have been seriously infringed. A product can be evaluated by reviews and ratings objectively. However, the topics of reviews are diverse while customers tend to focus on only a few aspects, and many reviews have wrong scores that are inconsistent with the content. Natural language processing (NLP) is helpful in mining the opinion of reviews automatically. In this paper, the goal is to improve fake product detection through text classification technology. Precisely, we use CNN and LSTM models to judge whether the review is quality related or not, which can remove useless reviews, and aspect-based sentiment analysis with an attention mechanism to determine the sentiment polarity of the concerning aspect to get ratings for different aspects. We experiment on the Self-Annotated datasets and results show that by using text classification technology, the performance of fake product detection can be greatly improved.

Keywords: Fake product detection · Text classification · Natural Language Processing

1 Introduction

The number of counterfeit products is sharply increasing, which has posed a serious threat to consumers. The research on fake product detection is particularly important. Most of the researches focus mainly on the attributes of products, such as price, brand, and logo [11, 12, 14, 15]. In this paper, we focus on text classification-related algorithm and we extract the features from reviews to determine whether a product is counterfeit or not.

The online reviews are vague and likely to contain linguistic cues associated with deception [1]. In this paper, we find there are two common characteristics of online reviews: 1) The content of reviews is irrelevant to the quality of the corresponding product. As shown in Example 1, the sentiment polarity is positive while the topic is service instead of quality. This part of the reviews has little help in fake product detection. 2) Reviews have the wrong scores. Customers are often asked for a rating when giving reviews. It is observed that scores for many reviews are default, which makes a lot of

Y. Yang et al. (Eds.): ICCC 2020, LNCS 12408, pp. 39–49, 2020.
https://doi.org/10.1007/978-3-030-59585-2_4

negative reviews with high scores (Example 2). In this paper, we use text classification to remove the quality-unrelated reviews and determine the scores for each aspect of the product, then we combine the product features and review features to detect the fake products.

	content	score
1.	Thoughtful and enthusiastic seller	5
2.	The paste is shaking and cannot be used normally, it is too fake	5

Fig. 1. Examples of online reviews. 1) The topic is service and is nothing to do with quality. 2) The polarity and scores are inconsistent.

Text classification, as one of the key tasks of natural language processing, can extend many sub-tasks, such as spam filtering, sentiment analysis [2], and so on. Recently, with the rapid development of pre-trained word embedding [3, 4], deep learning-based methods have achieved good performance in many text classification tasks [5, 6]. Word embedding, which is continuous vector representations of words from very large data sets, can capture the syntactic regularities and be used to measure the relatedness.

To capture the contextual information, Recurrent Neural Network (RNN) [7] encodes a text word by word and updates the hidden state to store information of the previous text. However, standard RNN has the problem of gradient vanishing, and Long Short-term Memory Network (LSTM) [8] were designed to combat vanishing gradients through a gating mechanism, which is among the most widely used models in Deep Learning for NLP today.

Inspired by human attention, attention mechanisms can be used to improve the ability of the model to focus on the key part of text [9]. In Neural Machine Translation (NMT), attention allows the model to learn alignments and has been proven to be greatly successful [10]. In this paper, we add attention mechanisms to aspect-based sentiment analysis to explore the important information of the review given aspect.

The contributions of this paper can be summarized as follows:

- We incorporate text classification into fake product detection. Our proposed method can capture the features of multiple aspects from quality-related reviews to overcome the problems in which the score and sentiment of review are inconsistent.
- We conduct experiments on three Self-Annotated datasets. The results show that our method has an improvement in different categories of products.

2 Related Work

Fake Product Detection. Features in fake product detection can be from different dimensions. Dong et al. [11] extracted features from three dimensions that are reviewer, commodity, and review, which can be applied to the recognition of cheater in Taobao. Wang et al. [12] created an algorithm called Iterative Computation Framework (ICF) to calculate the reliability of reviews, reviewers, and stores, and explore the dependencies between the three. Wahyuni et al. [14] utilized text mining techniques and FP-Growth [13] and proposed an ICF++ system to have better accuracy. Aradhana et al. [15] detected fake products by the concept which the authenticity of the product can be provided with invisible and visible watermarking.

Fake Review Detection. Reviews are an important indicator to determine whether the product is fake or not [16]. With the development of NLP, many approaches attempt to get features from reviews [17–21]. Heydari et al. [22] utilized time series to employ the rating deviation, content-based factors, and activeness of reviewers effectively and propose a robust fake review detection system. Bag-of-words can be used to eliminate fake reviews and determine the sentiment polarity for genuine reviews [23]. Jacob et al. [24] used three different algorithms including neural networks (CNN and RNN model) to explore unfair and fair positive and negative reviews. Jay et al. [25] exploited behavioral feature of reviewers and selected feature set containing a contextual feature which captures text similarity between reviews of a reviewer. However, these methods treat reviews as a whole, ignoring the weight and sentiment of different aspects within the reviews.

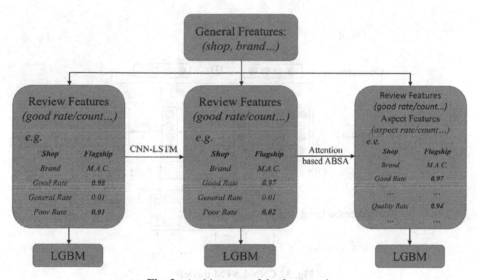

Fig. 2. Architecture of the framework

3 Method

Customers always evaluate the risk of a product from the reviews. However, the reviews on e-commerce often involve multiple aspects, such as the Quality, Logistics, and Service, and the ratings are always the default regardless of content. Reviews that are not related to quality or rated incorrectly are hardly helpful for fake detection. This section introduces methods of filtering reviews with text classification. Figure 2 shows the architecture of the framework. The base model uses the general features and review features directly to detect the fake products by the method of 3.3. Considering the length of reviews is always short, and we can determine whether it is related to quality from keywords. We use the CNN-LSTM model to get the degree related to quality and remove the quality-unrelated reviews, then we recalculate the review features to train the LGBM model. Further, we use attention-based LSTM for aspect-level sentiment classification to get the sentiment polarity for the concerned aspect as the complementary aspect features. At the end of this section, we introduce the method of fake product detection incorporated with text classification.

3.1 CNN-LSTM

Convolutional neural networks (CNN) have been widely used in text classification tasks due to the capability of feature extraction [5]. It can well capture the key parts for classification. However, it cannot characterize the temporal dependency in sequence data. To overcome this issue, we combine CNN and LSTM to further improve the representation ability of the model. Figure 3 illustrates the architecture of the model.

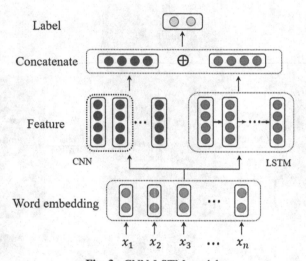

Fig. 3. CNN-LSTM model.

The input of the model is a review, which is a sequence of words $x = (x_1, \ldots, x_n)$. A convolution kernel $w \in R^{h*d}$ is used in a window of length h to capture the feature c with a local length h. Using it in the possible windows $\{x_{1:h}, x_{2:h+1}, \ldots, x_{n-h+1:n}\}$ of the input sequence, we can get the feature map of length h (Eq. (1)). A max-pooling layer is employed to automatically extracts the key features in text classification (Eq. (2)).

$$c_i = f(w \cdot x_{i:i+h-1} + b) \tag{1}$$

$$c = \max(c_1, \ldots, c_{n-h+1}) \tag{2}$$

To overcome the gradient vanishing problems, we use LSTM [8] with three gates and a memory cell to capture the long-term dependencies, the cell state can be computed as follows:

$$i = \sigma\left(x_t U^i + h_{t-1} W^i\right) \tag{3}$$

$$f = \sigma\left(x_t U^f + h_{t-1} W^f\right) \tag{4}$$

$$o = \sigma\left(x_t U^o + h_{t-1} W^o\right) \tag{5}$$

$$g = \tanh\left(x_t U^g + h_{t-1} W^g\right) \tag{6}$$

$$c_t = c_{t-1} \circ f + g \circ i \tag{7}$$

$$h_t = \tanh(c_t) \circ o \tag{8}$$

We concatenate the feature of CNN and the last hidden state h_n of LSTM. The experiment shows that it works better if we concatenate the sum of words embedding to get the final representation. A linear layer coverts the representation into a vector that is activated by Relu.

3.2 Attention-Based ABSA

To get the sentiment polarity of different aspects, we have aspect embedding a_i for the i-th aspect and use attention mechanism to focus on the key part of the review [26]. As shown in Fig. 4, we first use LSTM to encode the input review. We compute the attention scores α for each hidden state (Eq. (9)), which follow a softmax function to get the weight of the state. The context vector is obtained as the weighted average over all the hidden state (Eq. (10)).

$$\alpha_i = h_t^T \cdot a_i \tag{9}$$

$$c = \sum_{i=1}^{n} \alpha \cdot h_t \tag{10}$$

Same as before, we also concatenate the sum of words embedding and the context vector to get the final representation.

3.3 Fake Product Detection

We use multiple attributes of products as features to detect fakes, which are the brand of product, the shop name, the number of good (general or poor) reviews, and the rate of good (general or poor) reviews. First, we get the degree related to quality using the CNN-LSTM model and discard some unrelated reviews. Second, we use the Attention-based

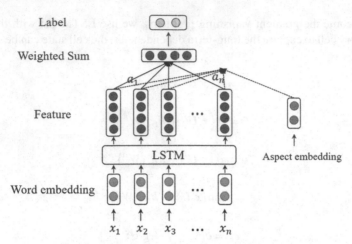

Fig. 4. Attention-based ABSA model.

ABSA model for the remaining reviews to get the sentiment polarity of the concerned aspect. For different categories, we design different three aspects. For example, lipstick has aspects of Quality, Experience, and Color. Because wrong-ratings reviews are always poor reviews with high scores, we also calculate the number and the rate of negative reviews related to each aspect as supplementary features. The features used are shown in Table 1.

Table 1. Features used for Lipsticks. We leave out shop name for privacy

Features	Description	Example
Brand	The brand of product	M.A.C
Shop	The shop name of product	–
Good Count(Rate)	Number/Rate of positive reviews	32 (0.8)
General Count(Rate)	Number/Rate of neutral reviews	5 (0.125)
Poor Count(Rate)	Number/Rate of negative reviews	3 (0.075)
Quality Count(Rate)	Number/Rate of negative reviews related to Quality Aspect	4 (0.1)
Experience Count(Rate)	Number/Rate of negative reviews related to Experience Aspect	6 (0.15)
Color Count(Rate)	Number/Rate of negative reviews related to Color Aspect	4 (0.1)

We use Light Gradient Boosting Machine (LightGBM) [27] to perform predictive analysis of fake products, which is an improvement on traditional GBDT with two new techniques: Gradient-based One-side Sampling (GOSS) and Exclusive Feature Bundling (EFB). GOSS can avoid the influence of long-tail by eliminating a large amount of data with a smaller gradient while still get comparable performance. EFB is designed to determine which features are used for fusion to get better performance. Besides, LightGBM uses Histogram algorithm for training speed and memory.

4 Experiments

4.1 Dataset

We evaluate our method on the Self-Annotated Fake Product Dataset from JD e-commerce[1]. To better process the reviews, we additionally develop a Quality Theme Dataset and an Aspect-based Sentiment Classification Dataset. The Fake Product Dataset consists of cross-border products and corresponding attributes, such as brand, the number of good reviews. Quality Theme Dataset and Aspect-based Sentiment Classification Dataset consist of reviews from products in Fake Product Dataset. Quality Theme Dataset also includes the labels for whether each review is related to quality and the Aspect-based Sentiment Classification Dataset contains the aspects of reviews and corresponding polarities. Table 2 shows a summary of datasets.

Table 2. A summary of the datasets, including the number of entries in each dataset, the number of brands and shops, and the number of each aspect entries. {$Qu., Ex., Ef., Co., Da., St.$} refer to {$quality, experience, effect, color, date, style$}.

Dataset	Num(Fake)	Brand	Shop	Asp_1	Asp_2	Asp_3
Lipsticks	968(258)	22	122	Qu.(905)	Ex.(580)	Co.(553)
Milk	882(117)	17	131	Qu.(1173)	Ef.(365)	Da.(195)
Shoes	642(151)	12	38	Qu.(1166)	Ex.(682)	St.(398)

Fake Product Dataset. Consisting of three different types of cross-border products, including Lipstick, Milk Powder, and shoes. Each product, including at least one review, is manually labeled and voted by three professionals to get labels.

Quality Theme Dataset. For each category of products, we develop a review dataset with a size of 3000, whose label is to determine whether the review is related to Quality. Review data is randomly drawn from the review database of the corresponding product. To balance the positive and negative samples, we deliberately select more reviews with lower ratings.

Aspect-Based Sentiment Classification Dataset. We have three aspects of each Fake Product datasets. Lipsticks dataset contains Quality, Experience, and Color. Milk Powders dataset contains Quality, Effect, and Date. Shoes dataset contains Quality, Experience, and Style. Sentiment polarity is labeled as positive and negative for each aspect within a review.

---

[1] https://www.jd.hk/.

4.2 Experiment Settings

We use jieba to segment the words in reviews and remove Emoji. All Fake Product Datasets are separated by 80% as the training set and keep the remaining as the testing set. The evaluation metric is the precision of fake products.

We use Tencent AI Lab Embedding [28] with a size of 200 for review classification, which is over 8 million Chinese words and phrases. The other parameters are initialized by sampling from a uniform distribution $G(0, 0.1)$. The hidden size of all neural network is 200. The kernel size of CNN is 3, 5, 7 with the number of 50. We train all models with a batch size of 8 and the learning rate of 0.005 for AdaGrad. For LightGBM, we use GridSearch to find the best parameters. Each aspect is considered negative if the threshold is over 0.9 for the improvement of precision. The threshold for fake product detection is 0.6 for Milk Powders and 0.7 for Lipsticks and Shoes.

4.3 Results and Analysis

For fake product detection, what we are most concerned about is precision. To demonstrate the effectiveness of the proposed method, we also provided recall and F1-score (Table 3, 4, 5).

Table 3. Results on fake product detection for Lipsticks datasets. Best scores are in bold

Models	Precision	Recall	F1-score
Baseline	0.811	0.462	0.588
+ CNN-LSTM	0.879	0.530	0.662
+ Att-based ABSA	**0.895**	**0.592**	**0.713**

Table 4. Results on fake product detection for Shoes datasets. Best scores are in bold

Models	Precision	Recall	F1-score
Baseline	0.857	0.508	0.637
+ CNN-LSTM	0.882	0.564	0.688
+ Att-based ABSA	**0.902**	**0.593**	**0.715**

The base model uses raw reviews to calculate the number and rate of good/general/poor reviews. Because there are a large number of default reviews with 5-score, e.g. "This user did not fill in the review content", and some quality-unrelated reviews (Example 1), which will make the good rate very high and further disturb the performance. When incorporating the CNN-LSTM component into the framework, this part of reviews will be removed and the feature of reviews (Table 1) will be revised. Precision in the three datasets has an improvement of 6.8%, 3.8%, and 19.1%, respectively. We investigate why Milk Powders has a large improvement compared to the other

Table 5. Results on fake product detection for Milk Powders datasets. Best scores are in bold

Models	Precision	Recall	F1-score
Baseline	0.704	0.501	0.585
+ CNN-LSTM	0.895	0.658	0.758
+ Att-based ABSA	**0.908**	**0.686**	**0.781**

two datasets. In particular, reviews in Milk Powder describe more about Logistics than Quality. Using CNN-LSTM will greatly reduce the effect of Logistics-related reviews on fake detection.

Att-base ABSA is to revise the reviews with wrong scores. As shown in Fig. 1, the sentiment polarity of Example 2 is negative for aspect term Quality and Experience. The attention mechanism can capture the important parts from the whole review for different aspects. Our method determines the sentiment polarity of both aspects as negative, so the corresponding counter is incremented. By adding aspect features, we have an improvement of 1.6%, 2.0% and 1.3% with regard to Lipstick, Shoes and Milk Powders respectively.

5 Conclusion

We incorporate text classification into fake product detection. The key idea is to determine whether the reviews are quality-related and the sentiment polarity of the concerned aspect. The experiment demonstrates that our method outperforms the base model in three datasets.

Acknowledgements. This work was partially supported by Key Technologies Research and Development Program of Shenzhen JSGG20170817140856618, Shenzhen Foundational Research Funding JCYJ20180507183527919, National Natural Science Foundation of China 61632011, 61876053.

References

1. Anderson, E., Simester, D.I.: Reviews without a purchase: low ratings, loyal customers, and deception. J. Mark. Res. **51**(3), 249–269 (2014)
2. Nasukawa, T., Yi, J.: Sentiment analysis: capturing favorability using natural language processing. In: Proceedings of the 2nd International Conference on Knowledge Capture, pp. 70–77 (2003)
3. Mikolov, T., Sutskever, I., Chen, K.: Distributed representations of words and phrases and their compositionality. In: Proceedings of the Conference and Workshop on Neural Information Processing Systems, pp. 3111–3119 (2013)
4. Mikolov, T., Yih, W.-T., Zweig, G.: Linguistic regularities in continuous space word representations. In: HLT-NAACL, pp. 746–751 (2013)

5. Kim, Y.: Convolutional neural networks for sentence classification. In: Proceedings of the 2014 Conference on Empirical Methods in Natural Language Processing, pp. 1746–1751 (2014)

6. Lai, S., Xu, L., Liu, K.: Recurrent convolutional neural networks for text classification. In: Proceedings of the Twenty-Ninth AAAI Conference on Artificial Intelligence, pp. 2267–2273 (2015)

7. Mikolov, T., Kombrink, S., Burget, L., et al.: Extensions of recurrent neural network language model. In: Proceedings of the International Conference on Acoustics, Speech, and Signal Processing, pp. 5528–5531 (2011)

8. Sundermeyer, M., Schlüter, R., Ney, H.: LSTM neural networks for language modeling. In: Proceedings of 13th Annual Conference of the International Speech Communication Association, pp. 194–197 (2012)

9. Hermann, K.M., Koisk, T., Grefenstette, E., et al.: Teaching machines to read and comprehend (2015)

10. Luong, M.T., Pham, H., Manning, C.D.: Effective approaches to attention-based neural machine translation. In: Proceedings of the 2015 Conference on Empirical Methods in Natural Language Processing, pp. 1412–1421 (2015)

11. Dong, B., Liu, Q., Fu, Y., Zhang, L.: A research of taobao cheater detection. In: Li, H., Mäntymäki, M., Zhang, X. (eds.) I3E 2014. IAICT, vol. 445, pp. 338–345. Springer, Heidelberg (2014). https://doi.org/10.1007/978-3-662-45526-5_31

12. Guan, W., Sihong, X., Bing, L., et al.: Review graph based online store review spammer detection. In: Proceeding ICDM 2011 Proceedings of the 2011 IEEE 11th International Conference on Data Mining, pp. 1242–1247 (2011)

13. Fournier-Viger, P., Gomariz Gueniche, T.A., Soltani, A., et al.: SPMF: a Java open-source pattern mining library. J. Mach. Learn. Res. (JMLR) 15(1), 3389–3393 (2014)

14. Wahyuni, E., Djunaidy, A.: Fake review detection from a product review using modified method of iterative computation framework. In: MATEC Web of Conferences (2016)

15. Behura, A., Behura, A., Das, H.: Counterfeit product detection analysis and prevention as well as prepackage coverage assessment using machine learning. In: Das, H., Pattnaik, P.K., Rautaray, S.S., Li, K.-C. (eds.) Progress in Computing, Analytics and Networking. AISC, vol. 1119, pp. 483–496. Springer, Singapore (2020). https://doi.org/10.1007/978-981-15-2414-1_49

16. Choudhury, M., Srinivasan, K.: An overview into the aspects of fake product reviews, its manipulation, and its effects and monitoring (2019)

17. Sinha, A., Arora, N., Singh, S., et al.: Fake product review monitoring using opinion mining. Int. J. Pure Appl. Math. 119(12), 13203–13208 (2018)

18. Li, L.-Y., Qin, B., Liu, T.: Survey on fake review detection research. Jisuanji Xuebao/Chinese J. Comput. 41(4), 946–968 (2018)

19. Shaohua, J., Xianguo, Z., Xinyue, W., et al.: Fake reviews detection based on LDA, pp. 280–283 (2018)

20. Neha, S., Anala, A.: Fake review detection using classification. Int. J. Comput. Appl. 180(50), 16–21 (2018)

21. Baraithiya, H., Pateriya, R.K.: Classifiers ensemble for fake review detection. Int. J. Innov. Technol. Explor. Eng. 8(4), 730–736 (2019)

22. Heydari, A., Tavakoli, M., Salim, N.: Detection of fake opinions using time series. Expert Syst. Appl. 58, 83–92 (2016)

23. Punde, A., Ramteke, S., Shinde, S., et al.: Fake product review monitoring & removal and sentiment analysis of genuine reviews. Int. J. Eng. Manage. Res. 9(2), 107–110 (2019)

24. Jacob, M.S., Rajendran, S., Michael Mario, V., Sai, K.T., Logesh, D.: Fake product review detection and removal using opinion mining through machine learning. In: Kumar, L.A.,

Jayashree, L.S., Manimegalai, R. (eds.) AISGSC 2019 2019, pp. 587–601. Springer, Cham (2020). https://doi.org/10.1007/978-3-030-24051-6_55

25. Kumar, J.: Fake review detection using behavioral and contextual features (2020)
26. Wang, Y., Huang, M., Zhu, X., Zhao, L.: Attention-based LSTM for aspect-level sentiment classification, pp. 606-615 (2016)
27. Guo, L.K., Qi, M., Finley, T., et al.: LightGBM: a highly efficient gradient boosting decision tree. In: 31st Conference on Neural Information Processing Systems, pp. 1–9 (2017)
28. Song, Y., Shi, S., Li, J., et al.: Directional skip-gram: explicitly distinguishing left and right context for word embeddings. In: NAACL (2018)

A Dual Layer Regression Model
for Cross-border E-commerce Industry Sale
and Hot Product Prediction

Wangda Luo, Hang Su, Yuhan Liu, and Ruifeng Xu[✉]

Harbin Institute of Technology (Shenzhen), Shenzhen 518055, China
luowangda_hitsz@163.com, suhang_hitsz@163.com,
liuyuhan_hitsz@163.com, xuruifeng@hit.edu.cn

Abstract. We introduce a novel regression model for time series forecasting in the cross-border e-commerce domain. In this paper, we present a new regression model for industry sale prediction (ISP) and hot product prediction (HPP) in the cross-border e-commerce domain. E-commerce products contain many attributes which may benefit to the final prediction performance. Based on this assumption, the proposed model employs a novel dual layer regression architecture to improve the generalization by capturing correlation between the historical data and future data, as well as enhancing the relationship of extracted features and target values. Besides, to verify the effectiveness of the proposed model, we establish two cross-border e-commerce datasets about imported lipsticks and shoes. The experimental results demonstrate that our proposed model achieves impressive results compared to a number of competitive baselines and the precision of hot product prediction reached 90%.

Keywords: Time series forecasting · Regression · Dual layer architecture

1 Introduction

In recent years, cross-border e-commerce has become a hot economical topic [26]. A professional online platform[1] estimates that the total value of the cross-border e-commerce market in 2019 is 826 billion dollars, and the total number of customers has reached 848 million. Predicting the future status of cross-border e-commerce industry and hot products have become the point of interest for every merchant [25]. We treat e-commerce **I**ndustry **S**ale **P**rediction (ISP) and **H**ot **P**roduct **P**rediction (HPP) are two sub-tasks of **T**ime **S**eries **F**orecasting (TSF [7, 9]). In these two tasks, the main research goal is to explore the possible trends of the industry and hot commodities in the future by leveraging the historical data of commodities and industries.

TSF has been applied in various aspects of our daily life, such as sale forecasting [27, 28], temperature prediction [29, 30], stock price prediction [31, 32] and other areas. Both traditional machine learning methods [7, 9] and deep learning models [19, 24, 32]

---

[1] https://www.invespcro.com/blog/cross-border-shopping/.

© Springer Nature Switzerland AG 2020
Y. Yang et al. (Eds.): ICCC 2020, LNCS 12408, pp. 50–61, 2020.
https://doi.org/10.1007/978-3-030-59585-2_5

have been developed to improve the robustness and effectiveness of time series models. We accumulate some experience from these works and using it to the cross-border e-commerce domain.

The task can be addressed through regression approaches. Under the supervised learning framework, the future value is predicted by the history feature. Linear regression or recurrent neural networks are common ways to obtain possible future sales volume for industry and the product. Although the above method is feasible, the generalization ability of the model is affected because, under the long-term relationship, the feature at each time points will be weakened layer by layer. To improve the program, we propose a dual-layer regression model to enhance the impact of feature relationships at each point in time. The dual-layer regression model consists of two components which are called the first layer regression and the second layer regression. Concretely, for the first layer regression, we build a time series regression model to capture the correlation between the history feature and future features. For the second layer, we propose a feature regression model to enhance the relation of feature and target in each time point.

Specifically, our contributions are two folds:

- We construct two datasets for industry sale prediction and hot product prediction in the cross-border e-commerce domain.
- We develop a dual-layer regression model which effectively combines time-series relationship with attributes features. Several experimental results reveal that the dual-layer regression model is superior to several strong baselines.

The rest of the paper is organized as follows: in Sect. 2, existing TSF methods are presented; Sect. 3 describes the whole process of dataset construction for two sub-tasks; our proposed model and several model details are introduced in Sect. 4; complicated experiments and analysis are illustrated in Sect. 5; finally we get our conclusion in Sect. 6.

2   Related Work

Traditional machine learning approaches perform well in many TSF tasks. Due to their unique statistical properties, ARIMA [7] and ARMA [9] become one of the most popular methods applied for TSF. [1] applies an autoregression-based linear model to predict the influenza-like illness ratio in Google Trends Dataset [2]. [5] develops an enhanced linear regression model with external signals for the same dataset. Online ARMIA is proposed by [3] to ensure full information online optimization for the ARMIA model. It performs well in the private cars registration dataset and daily index of Dow Jones Industrial Average dataset. [4] proposes BHT-ARMIA which combines multi-way delay embedding transform with tensor decomposition for TSF. [6] focuses on non-stationary time series and develops Harmonic Recurrent Process for forecasting. [8] builds the multilinear orthogonal autoregressive model the multilinear constrained autoregressive model to solve the problem of high-order time series forecasting.

Recent years, Recurrent Neural Network (RNN) and Convolutional Neural Network (CNN) have shown great power in natural language processing [16, 17], computer vision

[12, 13] and other scientific fields. And plenty of deep learning techniques have also been applied to TSF. Based on Gated Recurrent Units (GRU [11]), [14] develops GRU-D to explore the missing patterns for those missing values and improves the prediction performance. [15] proposes a model named LSTNet utilizing Long-Short Time Memory units (LSTM [10]) and CNN to analyze multi-variate time series. DeepAR [23] and DeepState [24] are two recently proposed RNN-based models. DeepState parametrizes a linear state-space model with a jointly-learned RNN and DeepAR is an auto-regressive recurrent network. Besides, inspired by the great success of attention mechanism [20, 21] in several sequential learning tasks. [18, 19] build transformer-based deep neural networks and their experimental results prove the effectiveness. Transformer [22] is a novel network architecture that leverages multi-head attention for sequence processing.

3 Dataset Construction

We collect and organize lipsticks and shoes sale data from the NetEase Kaola platform[2] in recent two years. We build two kinds of datasets about imported lipsticks and imported shoes: (1) industry datasets (see Table 1) which are used for ISP; (2) hot product datasets from (see Table 2) for HPP.

Table 1. Statistics of the two industry datasets

Dataset name	Train	Test
Lipsticks	509	217
Shoes	509	217

Table 2. Statistics about hot products of the two datasets

Dataset name	Month	Hot products	Others
Lipsticks	October	72	128
	November	67	133
	December	59	141
Shoes	October	39	161
	November	35	165
	December	31	169

We leverage the scrapy[3] framework to crawl basic information of each imported lipsticks and shoes in the platform and further get their review information according to

[2] https://www.kaola.com/.
[3] https://scrapy.org/.

the platform API. Respectively, there are 3802 lipstick commodities with 433 k reviews and 14360 shoe commodities with 178 k reviews.

In each dataset, the basic features of each commodity have more than 20 kinds and the important features have product name, product type, product brand, product price, number of reviews, number of positive words, number of negative words, product origin, number of likes, festival distance, months, workday and product score.

We use the number of product reviews as the sales volume of a corresponding product. We take sales volume as the target value, and other attributes of a product (see above) as features to build industry datasets. Table 1 illustrates the sale information of the imported lipstick and imported shoe industry from January 1, 2018 to December 31, 2019. We separate the data into a training set of 70% and a test set of 30% (window_size = 4). For hot product dataset, we first calculate the product data in October, November, and December of 2019, and then use the top 10% of products with sales data as hot products. Finally, we randomly extract 200 items from them (see Table 2).

4 Methodology

4.1 Problem Description

For ISP, the target goal is to predict future sales volume as accurately as possible according to known history time-series information. The time-series data contain N daily time point $\{x_1, x_2, \ldots, x_N\}$ and every time point has M related features $\{a_1, a_2, \ldots, a_M\}$. The task utilizes T history time point $x_1, x_2, \ldots, x_T$ for supervised training and predicts the value of future time points $x_{T+1}, x_{T+2}, \ldots, x_N$ based on the trained supervised model. For HPP, the basic goal is the same as ISP except that it is for products rather than industries. Then we need to judge whether each product is hot-selling based on predicted value.

4.2 Dual Layer Regression Model

We propose a dual-layer regression model that is effective and reasonable for TSF in e-commerce. The proposed model can retain more internal and external features at each time point. Besides the long-distance information loss and time lag caused by the single regression model are reduced. The characteristics of the original structure of each layer will be described as follows:

The First Layer Regression. The main parts of the first layer is a regression model based on time series relation. The goal of this layer is to learn the temporal relationship of historical sequences and predict future sequences. For the first layer, we extracted each feature at each time point $x_i = \{a_1^i, a_2^i, \ldots, a_M^i\}$ and establish a multi-dimensional feature sequence $< x_1, x_2, \ldots, x_t >$ (here window size is t) as the input of the regression model RE I (see Fig. 1) to predict the time point $x_{t+1} = \{a_1^{t+1}, a_2^{t+1}, \ldots, a_M^{t+1}\}$. For the regression model, we adopt the LSTM as the regression model RE I, which consisted of cell status c_t, input gate i_t, forget gate f_t and output gate h_t and the model compute is shown in Eq. 1. LSTM was proposed by [15] and the model can deal with the gradient explosion and gradient vanishing problem caused by traditional recurrent neural networks and retain more temporal information, so the model widely used in time series predict task.

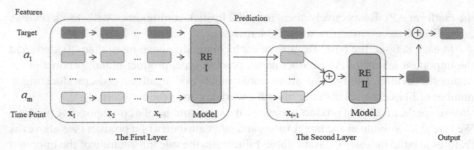

Fig. 1. The dual-layer regression model. RE I and RE II is a regression model

$$i_t = \sigma(W_i \cdot [h_{t-1}, x_t] + b_i)$$
$$f_t = \sigma(W_f \cdot [h_{t-1}, x_t] + b_f)$$
$$\tilde{c}_t = \tanh(W_c \cdot [h_{t-1}, x_t] + b_c)$$
$$c_t = f_t * C_{t-1} + i_t * \tilde{c}_t$$
$$o_t = \sigma(W_o \cdot [h_{t-1}, x_t] + b_o)$$
$$h_t = o_t * \tanh(c_t) \tag{1}$$

The Second Layer Regression. The purpose of this layer is to discover the relationship between related attributes and target value at each time point. The input data of the second layer comes from future predict results $x_{t+1} = \left\{ a_1^{t+1}, a_2^{t+1}, \ldots, a_M^{t+1} \right\}$ by the first layer regression (see Fig. 1) because we can't obtain the related features at future time points. The Elastic Net [36] is adopted as the regression model RE II. The model is a linear regression model using L1 and L2 priors as regularization matrices, which is very effective when multiple features in the time point are related to the target value.

4.3 Model Training

In order to train RE I, we use Adam optimizer to improve the RE I model parameters and utilize mean-square-errors (MSE) as the model loss function to evaluate the model performance. The model parameters w compute is shown in Eq. 2 and parameter g is time gradient, m and v is Exponential moving average of gradient and gradient squared.

$$g_t = \nabla_w L(w_{t-1})$$
$$m_t = \beta_1 m_{t-1} + (1 - \beta_1)g_t$$
$$v_t = \beta_2 v_{t-1} + (1 - \beta_2)g_t^2$$
$$\hat{m}_t = m_t/(1 - \beta_1^t)$$
$$\hat{v}_t = v_t/(1 - \beta_2^t)$$
$$w_t = w_{t-1} - a * \hat{m}_t/(\sqrt{\hat{v}_t} + \varepsilon) \tag{2}$$

For the second regression RE II training process, we utilize the ElasticNet loss function and it effectively limits the model parameters to a suitable range, thereby preventing the model from overfitting, which compute is shown in Eq. 3.

$$L(\tilde{w}) = \min_{w} \left[\sum_{i=1}^{n} (\tilde{w}^T x - \hat{y})^2 + \lambda_1 \sum_{j=1}^{n} \|w\| + \lambda_2 \|w\|_2^2 \right] \tag{3}$$

5 Experimentation

5.1 Experimental Settings

Parameter Setting. For the first layer regression, we set Adam optimizer with learning rate $\alpha = 0.01$, exponential decay coefficient $\beta_1 = 0.9$, $\beta_2 = 0.999$ and $\varepsilon = 10^{-8}$, and iteratively train the model 1000 times to minimize the model loss. For the second layer regression, we set the model parameter with $a = 0.0004$ and $L1\_ratio = 0.8$.

Metric. For evaluation, we compute the mean absolute percentage error (MAPE) between actual sequence data y_i and predicted data $\hat{y}_i$ and n is sequence length and output 1-MAPE as the final evaluation result, which is shown in Eq. 4. In order to better evaluate the performance of TSF, we divided the test data sets of Lipsticks and Shoes into 10%, 30%, 50% and 100% to evaluate the model's prediction effect in the early, middle, and late stages.

$$1-MAPE = 1 - \frac{100\%}{n} \sum_{i=1}^{n} \left| \frac{\hat{y}_i - y_i}{\hat{y}_i} \right| \tag{4}$$

In hot product prediction, we adopt accuracy, precision, recall and Micro-F1 score as the metrics.

Baselines and Comparisons. In our study, the following models were compared:

- **LR, Lasso, Ridge, ElasticNet:** They are a traditional linear regression model based on the least square method. Lasso Regression is a linear regression method that uses L1-regularization and in the study, we set parameter $a = 0.003$ in order to keep the best performance. Ridge regression is a linear regression method that uses L2-regularization. The ElasticNet is a power linear regression model based on the combination between the L1 and L2 regularization and in that study, we set the parameters $a = 0.0004$ and $L1\_ratio = 0.8$ for better status.
- **GBR, LightGBM:** They are powerful TSF integrated models based on machine learning. Gradient boost regression (GBR) is an integrated model which fit performance with multiple weak models and LightGBM [34] is a gradient boost framework which is based on decision trees. in the study we set these model parameters with n_estimator = 20 and max_deep = 3.

- **SARIMA:** Seasonal Autoregressive Integrated Moving Average (SARIMA [35]) is a powerful Statistical regression model for TSF. In the study, we set parameter (p,d,q) = (2,1,1) and seasonal parameter s = (1,1,1,26).
- **LSTM, Seq2Seq:** They are RNN models. Seq2seq model [33] is a encode-decode structure model which can encode history series information and in that study, we set parameters lr = 0.0002, batch_size = 8, epoch = 20, input and output window size = 6 and 2.

In the above comparison models, unless otherwise specified, their parameters are set by default.

5.2 Results and Analysis

Industry Sale Volume Forecast. Table 3 shows the results of different models over Lipsticks and Shoes. From the results, we can see that the performance of our proposed model is better than other strong regression models in Lipsticks and our model also has a competitive result in Shoes. The reason may be that the internal relationship at each time point in the first-level regression is weakened under the long-term series, while the second layer regression fully considers the relationship between the related feature at each time point and the target sales volume, which mitigates the impact. The visualization is shown in Fig. 2. We can find that the model has a good fit.

Table 3. Performance of different models in Lipsticks and Shoes. Models are tested using 10%, 30%, 50% and 100% of the test sets.

Model	Lipsticks				Shoes			
	1-MAPE				1-MAPE			
	10%	30%	50%	100%	10%	30%	50%	100%
LR	88.88	90.01	89.71	85.85	87.91	88.05	87.63	83.77
Lasso	89.73	90.68	90.15	86.26	88.10	**88.06**	87.73	84.13
Ridge	88.89	90.01	89.17	85.86	87.27	87.08	86.84	83.95
ElasticNet	90.29	90.87	90.18	86.47	88.06	88.03	87.71	84.17
GBR	89.55	89.39	89.46	86.39	87.38	88.05	**87.77**	84.96
LightGBM	89.64	89.60	89.61	86.57	87.68	88.02	87.77	84.95
SARIMA	83.19	74.62	78.87	80.46	81.40	78.25	79.70	76.35
LSTM	86.82	89.09	89.61	87.08	86.77	86.92	86.93	83.78
Seq2seq	84.14	79.16	82.88	81.95	71.25	76.50	66.59	63.62
Our method	**90.48**	**91.51**	**91.12**	**88.85**	**89.36**	87.57	86.95	**85.22**

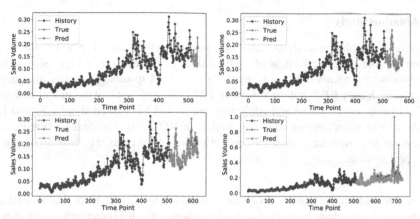

Fig. 2. Sequence prediction visualization over Lipstick. Models are tested using 10%, 30%, 50% and 100% of the test sets.

Hot Product Prediction. The results of hot product prediction in Lipsticks and Shoes are illustrated in Table 4. We predict the hot products in October, November, and December. Through our proposed model, we predict the total sales of different products in October, November, and December, and determine whether the predicted products are hot products based on the corresponding hot product sales threshold for the corresponding month (The hot product threshold for the corresponding month is predicted by the ElasticNet based on the hot commodity threshold from January 2019 to September 2019). Table 4 shows the result of different models over Lipsticks and Shoes. From the results, we proposed model has a strong performance in hot product prediction. The visualization is shown in Fig. 3, the model has a strong fit in these two datasets.

Table 4. The model performance about hot product prediction over Lipsticks and Shoes

Month	Lipsticks				Shoes			
	ACC	P	R	F1	ACC	P	R	F1
October	0.92	0.92	0.92	0.92	0.91	0.91	0.91	0.91
November	0.92	0.92	0.92	0.92	0.97	0.96	0.96	0.96
December	0.90	0.90	0.90	0.90	0.93	0.93	0.93	0.93

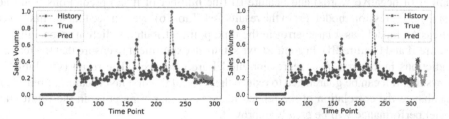

Fig. 3. Visualization about hot product prediction of Lipsticks and Shoes

5.3   Ablation Study

We perform an ablation analysis based on two industry datasets Lipsticks and Shoes. We first explore the effectiveness of each module of our dual-layer regression model. Table 5 shows the results. Taking model performance in Lipsticks dataset as an example, the model with only RE I performs worst in 10% and 30% test and the model with only RE II performs worst in 50% and 100% test. our model has gained about 2.34 and 1,17 percent improvement than the other two models in 100% test. The dual-layer regression structure we proposed does reduce the time series prediction error, which in turn improves model performance.

Table 5. The model performance over Lipsticks_Hot and Shoes_Hot. Only RE I utilize the timing relationship of sales volume to predict future sales volume. Only RE II represent merely uses the relationship of features to predict the future sales volume of product and note that the future feature input of RE II is obtained by RE I. RE I, RE II represents combine product features and timing relationship of sales volume to predict future sales volume.

	Lipsticks				Shoes			
	1-MAPE				1-MAPE			
	10%	30%	50%	100%	10%	30%	50%	100%
Only RE I	86.82	89.09	89.61	87.08	86.77	86.92	86.93	83.78
Only RE II	89.96	90.50	89.13	86.51	84.59	82.92	80.39	79.81
RE I, RE II	**90.48**	**91.51**	**91.12**	**88.85**	**89.36**	**87.57**	**86.95**	**85.22**

5.4   Limitations and Further Discussion

Our proposed model has shown great performance in both ISP and HHP tasks, but there is still plenty of potential improvement space and it has some shortages. The most obvious limitation is error propagation between the module layers. Due to relatively inaccurate predictions about different features from the first layer, the final prediction can be affected by those errors. To directly show the influence of error propagation, We first conduct experiments on Feature I (the number of positive words), Feature II (the number of negative words) and Feature III (the number of likes) predictions from the first layer regression model. From the results (see Table 6), we can see that the first layer regression model has a large error in the time point attribute prediction (especially on Feature II and Feature III). In contrast, we set up an experiment to ensure that the feature predictions in the first layer regression model are error-free. The result (see Table 7) shows that if it can be guaranteed to reduce the error of the first layer features prediction or enhance the correlation of the related features at each time point in the future, the model performance will be greatly improved.

Table 6. The features prediction by the first layer regression over Lipsticks and Shoes

	Lipsticks				Shoes			
	1-MAPE				1-MAPE			
	10%	30%	50%	100%	10%	30%	50%	100%
Feature I	85.50	85.20	85.78	85.92	84.41	82.94	81.52	79.46
Feature II	61.05	66.61	68.72	72.76	40.64	43.63	40.55	39.47
Feature III	66.98	64.53	65.57	56.89	28.80	38.04	34.76	4.95

Table 7. The Lossy and lossless performance of the model over Lipsticks and Shoes

	Lipsticks				Shoes			
	1-MAPE				1-MAPE			
	10%	30%	50%	100%	10%	30%	50%	100%
Our method	90.48	91.51	91.12	88.85	89.36	87.57	86.95	85.22
Our method + Not Features Loss	92.14	92.44	92.30	89.90	91.84	90.44	89.21	87.41

6 Conclusion

In this paper, we focus on industry sales volume prediction and hot product perdition. We first build two datasets from the e-commerce platform. Then we proposed a novel dual-layer regression model, which is based on the long short-term memory network as the first-level time series regression and the ElasticNet as the second-level feature regression. In the imported lipstick and shoe industry sales datasets, our proposed model performs better than other strong baseline models, and the ablation analysis proves that the dual-layer architecture can improve prediction performance. All those experiments show the effectiveness and robustness of our methods.

Acknowledgments. This work was partially supported by Key Technologies Research and Development Program of Shenzhen JSGG20170817140856618, Shenzhen Foundational Research Funding JCYJ20180507183527919, National Natural Science Foundation of China 61632011, 61876053.

References

1. Lazer, D., Kennedy, R., King, G., et al.: The parable of Google flu: traps in big data analysis. Science **343**(6176), 1203–1205 (2014)
2. Ginsberg, J., Mohebbi, M.H., Patel, R., et al.: Detecting influenza epidemics using search engine query data. Nature **457**(7232), 1012–1014 (2009)
3. Liu, C., Hoi, S.C., Zhao, P., et al.: Online ARIMA algorithms for time series prediction. In: National Conference on Artificial Intelligence, pp. 1867–1873 (2016)

4. Shi, Q., Yin, J., Cai, J., et al.: Block Hankel tensor ARIMA for multiple short time series forecasting. In: National Conference on Artificial Intelligence (2020)
5. Araz, O.M., Bentley, D., Muelleman, R.L., et al.: Using Google flu trends data in forecasting influenza-like-illness related ed visits in Omaha, Nebraska. Am. J. Emerg. Med. **32**(9), 1016–1023 (2014)
6. Zhang, S.Q., Zhou, Z.H.: Harmonic recurrent process for time series forecasting. In: European Conference on Artificial Intelligence (2020)
7. Box, G.E., Jenkins, G.M.: Some recent advances in forecasting and control. J. Roy. Stat. Soc. Ser. C (Appl. Stat.) **17**(2), 91–109 (1968)
8. Peiguang, J., Yuting, S., Xiao, J., et al.: High-order temporal correlation model learning for time-series prediction. IEEE Trans. Cybern. **49**, 1–13 (2018)
9. Box, G.E., Jenkins, G.M.: Time series analysis, forecasting and control. J. Am. Stat. Assoc. **134**(3) (1971)
10. Hochreiter, S., Schmidhuber, J.: Long short-term memory. Neural Comput. **9**(8), 1735–1780 (1997)
11. Cho, K., Van Merrienboer, B., Gulcehre, C., et al.: Learning phrase representations using rnn encoder-decoder for statistical machine translation. arXiv: Computation and Language (2014)
12. He, K., Zhang, X., Ren, S., et al.: Deep residual learning for image recognition. In: Computer Vision and Pattern Recognition, pp. 770–778 (2016)
13. Kim, Y.: Convolutional neural networks for sentence classification. In: Empirical Methods in Natural Language Processing, pp. 1746–1751 (2014)
14. Che, Z., Purushotham, S., Cho, K., et al.: Recurrent neural networks for multivariate time series with missing values. Sci. Rep. **8**(1), 6085 (2017)
15. Lai, G., Chang, W., Yang, Y., et al.: Modeling long- and short-term temporal patterns with deep neural networks. In: International ACM SIGIR Conference on Research and Development in Information Retrieval, pp. 95–104 (2018)
16. Mikolov, T., Karafiat, M., Burget, L., et al.: Recurrent neural network based language model. In: Conference of the International Speech Communication Association, pp. 1045–1048 (2010)
17. Du, J., Gui, L., He, Y., et al.: A convolutional attentional neural network for sentiment classification. In: International Conference on Security. IEEE (2018)
18. Li, S., Jin, X., Xuan, Y., et al.: Enhancing the locality and breaking the memory bottleneck of transformer on time series forecasting. In: Neural Information Processing Systems, pp. 5244–5254 (2019)
19. Neo, W., Bradley, G., Xue, B., et al.: Deep transformer models for time series forecasting: the influenza prevalence case. arXiv: Computation and Language (2020)
20. Bahdanau, D., Cho, K., Bengio, Y., et al.: Neural machine translation by jointly learning to align and translate. In: International Conference on Learning Representations (2015)
21. Chorowski, J., Bahdanau, D., Serdyuk, D., et al.: Attention-based models for speech recognition. In: Neural Information Processing Systems, pp. 577–585 (2015)
22. Vaswani, A., Shazeer, N., Parmar, N., et al.: Attention is all you need. In: Neural Information Processing Systems, pp. 6000–6010 (2017)
23. Salinas, D., Flunkert, V., Gasthaus, J., et al.: DeepAR: probabilistic forecasting with autoregressive recurrent networks. Int. J. Forecast. **36**, 1181–191 (2019)
24. Rangapuram, S.S., Seeger, M., Gasthaus, J., et al.: Deep state space models for time series forecasting. In: Neural Information Processing Systems, pp. 7785–7794 (2018)
25. Jian, L., Chunlin, L., Lanping, Z., et al.: Research on sales information prediction system of e-commerce enterprises based on time series model. Inf. Syst. E-Bus. Manage. (2019)
26. Charles, M.: Marketing and e-commerce as tools of development in the Asia-Pacific region: a dual path. Int. Market. Rev. **21**(3), 301–320 (2004)

27. Kechyn, G., Yu, L., Zang, Y., et al.: Sales forecasting using WaveNet within the framework of the Kaggle competition. arXiv: Learning (2018)
28. Choi, T., Yu, Y., Au, K., et al.: A hybrid SARIMA wavelet transform method for sales forecasting. Decis. Support Syst. **51**(1), 130–140 (2011)
29. Chen, S., Hwang, J.: Temperature prediction using fuzzy time series. Syst. Man Cybern. **30**(2), 263–275 (2000)
30. Xiao, C., Chen, N., Hu, C., et al.: Short and mid-term sea surface temperature prediction using time-series satellite data and LSTM-AdaBoost combination approach. Remote Sens. Environ. (2019)
31. Ariyo, A.A., Adewumi, A.O., Ayo, C.K., et al.: Stock price prediction using the ARIMA model. In: International Conference on Computer Modelling and Simulation, pp. 106–112 (2014)
32. Singh, R., Srivastava, S.: Stock prediction using deep learning. Multimed. Tools Appl. **76**(18), 18569–18584 (2017)
33. Sutskever, I., Vinyals, O., Le, Q.V., et al.: Sequence to sequence learning with neural networks. arXiv: Computation and Language (2014)
34. Ke, G., Meng, Q., Finley, T.W., et al.: LightGBM: a highly efficient gradient boosting decision tree. In: Neural Information Processing Systems, pp. 3149–3157 (2017)
35. Luo, C.S., Zhou, L.Y., Wei, Q.F.: Application of SARIMA model in cucumber price forecast. Appl. Mech. Mater. **373**, 1686–1690 (2013)
36. Zou, H., Hastie, T.: Addendum: regularization and variable selection via the elastic net. J. Roy. Stat. Soc. Ser. B **67**(5), 768–768 (2005)

End-to-End Nested Multi-Attention Network for 3D Brain Tumor Segmentation

Xinrui Zhuang and Yujiu Yang[✉]

Tsinghua Shenzhen International Graduate School, Tsinghua University,
Shenzhen, China
yang.yujiu@sz.tsinghua.edu.cn

Abstract. Utilizing the powerful feature learning ability of deep learning, researchers have proposed a variety of effective methods for brain tumor segmentation in three-dimensional medical images. However, the existing approaches often need to be processed in stages pipeline, without considering the anatomical nested structural characteristics of brain tumors, thus affecting the accuracy and efficiency of tumor segmentation. In this paper, we propose the Nested Multi-Attention mechanism **Network (NMA-Net)** tailored for brain tumors, which can effectively connect the sub-segmentation tasks of different organizations, and can directly conduct end-to-end training. By using the segmentation result of the tumor peripheral tissue as a kind of soft attention to the tumor segmentation task, it can make the subsequent network focus more on the region of interest, which makes it possible to obtain more accurate segmentation results. Besides, we transform multi-class segmentation tasks into multiple binary sub-segmentation tasks. Experiments on the BraTS'2017 Challenge Dataset show that the proposed **NMA-Net** framework is very suitable for organ tissue segmentation with nested anatomical structures. Here, our single-view model achieves the best segmentation performance compared with the exiting approaches, and the multi-view fusion model also achieves the state-of-the-art performance on the TC and ET sub-regions.

Keywords: Brain tumor segmentation · Nested network · Attention

1 Introduction

Accurate characterization and identification of different types of tissues are critical for the diagnosis of tumors and subsequent related treatments. In current clinical practice, the delineation of tumors in medical image is often done by a professional doctor or an experienced radiologist. However, medical images are different from traditional natural scenes 2D images, and the magnetic resonance imaging (MRI) or Computed Tomography (CT) is often required for the diagnosis of many tumors, preoperative planning and post-operative radiotherapy, so it requires higher segmentation performance. The manual segmentation

© Springer Nature Switzerland AG 2020
Y. Yang et al. (Eds.): ICCC 2020, LNCS 12408, pp. 62–76, 2020.
https://doi.org/10.1007/978-3-030-59585-2_6

of these generated 3D images is a labor-intensive, time-consuming, and costly task. Moreover, the judgment criteria of different operators for the same image are often not completely consistent, so the final segmentation result has a large inter-class and intra-class deviation.

The development of deep learning has greatly promoted the research on automatic segmentation in medical images, but the unique characteristics of medical images have added great difficulty to automate segmentation method. First, the boundary between different tumor substructures and other normal tissues are often ambiguous, there will be irregular discontinuities in the boundary in the low-level tumor images; secondly, the size, shape, position, contrast ingestion, etc. of the tumor also vary greatly among different patients, this limits the addition of some useful prior knowledge to the segmentation task.

Given the complexity of the task, much of the current work is done to solve the segmentation of multiple tumor substructures by designing a more powerful and complex model. There is also a lot of work to break down complex tasks, use multiple simple models to handle different subtasks, and finally cascaded them together, but one drawback to this cascaded network is that it is not an end-to-end network, therefore, the training and inference process will be less efficient. In addition, this decomposition of the overall task into several sub-tasks will lead to a serious drawback: although each sub-task can achieve local optimum, it can not achieve global optimum. Therefore, we propose an end-to-end model that transforms multiple tumor sub-region segmentation problems into multiple binary segmentation tasks, while utilizing the anatomic features of the tumors. The segmentation result of the peripheral edema region of the tumor was token as an attentional mechanism to the segmentation sub-task for the nuclear part of the tumor, and the segmentation result of the tumor core portion is also added to the segment of the edema region inside the tumor nucleus through the attention mechanism. By doing this, each sub-network will focus more on the different parts of the tumor for the region of interest, and the whole model is more efficient in the training process. We optimize the model as a whole so that we can coordinate each subtask to achieve global optimality.

In this paper, we propose an end-to-end framework with multi-attention, the contributions of this work can be summarized as follows:

- We propose an end-to-end network for multi-class 3D biomedical segmentation. We transform the segmentation problem of multiple complex sub-regions into different sub-tasks, then combine these sub-tasks together and optimize them as a whole, which can achieve global optimization while make each subnet focus more on the specific sub-region.
- We take attention approach to make full use of the structural features of tumor anatomy. The segmentation result of the peripheral edema region of the tumor was taken as an attentional mechanism to the segmentation sub-task for the nuclear part of the tumor, and the segmentation result of the tumor core portion is also added to the segment of the enhance region inside the tumor nucleus through the attention mechanism.

– Experimental results on BraTS'17 challenge demonstrate that our single
  model outperforms state-of-the-art 3D brain tumor segmentation methods
  with less input sequences.

2   Related Work

Deep learning algorithms, in particular convolutional neural networks, have
rapidly become a methodology of choice for analyzing medical images [12]. Different from previous generation models, which rely heavily on domain-specific
prior knowledge of health and tumor tissue appearance and complete the division
of tumor regions by utilizing anatomical structural features and the probability
distribution of tumors, the discriminant models represented by deep learning
are not dependent on hand-crafted features, but automatically learn a hierarchy of increasingly complex features directly from data [4]. The introduction of
fully convolutional networks (FCN) established a convolutional neural network
architecture that is widely used for the task of semantic segmentation. FCN can
produce a whole feature map with the same size of input images, rather than an
output class for only center point [17].

U-net [14] are another popular architecture in medical segmentation tasks,
which are also widely used in other semantic task. U-net merge feature maps
from the encoding path during the up-sampling process by skip connections
[3], which turn out to be crucial in the subsequent U-net variants structures.
Skip connections help the up-sampling path recover fine-grained information
from the down-sampling layers. However, these approach works on individual
2D slices without considering 3D contextual information. Tseng et al. leverage
convolutional LSTM to better exploit the spatial and sequential correlations of
consecutive slices [15].

3D U-net is able to exploit the available volumetric information of 3D images
by 3D convolution, and is widely used in volumetric medical image segmentation
task in the last two years [2]. In view of the complex structure and multiple
substructures of tumor tissue in medical images, the current segmentation of
3D medical images is mainly divided into two branches. One is to design a
more complex single model to improve the performance on complex tasks. For
example, introducing a residual connection based on 3D U-net [20]. This residual
short connection framework [6] not only improved the performance on the image
segmentation task by a wide margin, but also alleviated the degradation problem
found when an excessive amount of layers was used. What's more, the dense
connection structure is also added to construct a more representative network
[7,9]. However, one of the shortcomings of these models is that it cannot focus on
all subtasks at the same time, especially for the fuzzy organizational boundaries
and small regions, which usually have disappointing performance.

Another important branch is transforming the segmentation problem of multiple complex sub-regions into multiple different sub-tasks, and then optimize
each sub-task separately [1,17,19]. Rather than using a complicated model, these
works utilize multiple simple models to handle different subtasks and finally cascaded them together. One drawback to this cascaded network is that it is not

an end-to-end network, therefore, the training and inference process will be less efficient. The overall task is decomposed into several parts, although each sub-task can achieve local optimum, it cannot achieve global optimality. To avoid the aforementioned problem, it also inspires us to design a unified framework for making the solution as close as possible to the global optimum, through end-to-end training.

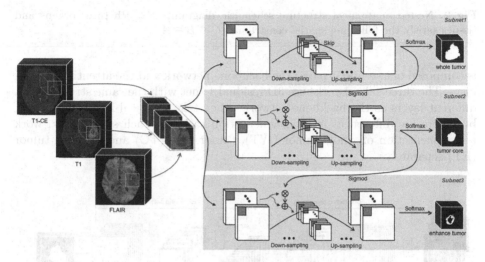

Fig. 1. The main architecture of our proposed end-to-end nested multi-attention network(**NMA-Net**). The three sub-nets use the same structure of 3D residual U-net with different layers. Between two adjacent sub-nets, we use the attention mechanism to connect. In our framework, we adopt cross-entropy as the loss function for all three sub-networks.

3 Nested Multi-Attention Network

3.1 Nested Organs Segmentation Problem

In the task of brain tumour segmentation, there is a nested spatial constraint relationship between the whole tumor (WT), the tumor core (TC) and the enhanced tumor (ET), that is , $ET \in TC \in WT$ as shown in Fig. 2. This segmentation task with the corresponding spatial constraints are called nested organizational segmentation problem.

3.2 Nested Multi-Attention Network Framework

In order to segment the brain tumor tissues with nested constraints, we propose a corresponding nested segmentation network framework (see Fig. 1). Our model

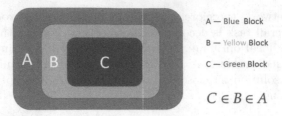

Fig. 2. Nested anatomical structure schematic diagram, in which three organs and tissues satisfy the following spatial constraints: $C \in B \in A$.

is composed of two major parts: the backbone network and the attention mechanism. The three subnetworks use 3D residual U-net with the same structure but different layers as the backbone network. They take identical input 3D images, but there are differences in the segmentation tasks for each subnetwork, work for segmentation of whole tumor (WT), tumor core (TC) and enhance tumor (ET) separately.

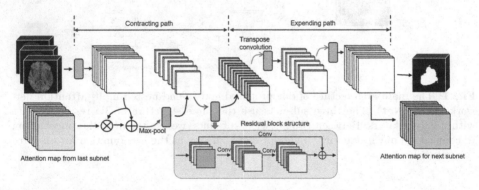

Fig. 3. Diagram of 3D residual U-net backbone network. All three sub-networks use the same structure, only the network depth is different, 4 times, 4 times, 3 times for three sub-networks respectively.

Backbone Networks: We adopt the 3D U-net as our basic structure, which has been proved can acquire better performance than original 2D U-net structure [2] in volumetric medical image segmentation task. In order to increase the learning ability of the network and prevent the gradient vanishing due to too many network layers, we added residual block structure to the 3D U-net (see Fig. 3.).

We use only one residual block at each layer, inside each residual block, we use batch normalization, ReLU activation function, $3 \times 3 \times 3$ convolution in turn. Note that different sub-regions have different voxel ratios in the training patches, for example enhance tumor (ET) only accounts for one-twentieth or even less of a single patch. We employ different network depths for different sub-networks, that is, the down-sampling multiples is different, 4 times, 4 times, 3 times for three sub-networks respectively.

Attention Mechanism: The segmentation task of tumor and other related lesions in medical images is different from traditional semantic segmentation, and it is necessary to understand the characteristics of its anatomical structure. According to the anatomical features of brain tumors, the tissues from the outside to the inside are whole tumor (WT), tumor core (TC) and enhanced tumor (ET) respectively, more detailed description can find in Sect. 4.1. Therefore, we introduce the attention mechanism, which can make better use of the mutual inclusion relationship between different brain tumor sub-regions.

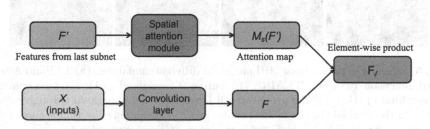

Fig. 4. Diagram of our attention module. The upper branch is used to obtain the attention map, The lower branch is the contracting path in next sub-network, $F(x)$ is the feature maps after the first residual block.

Our attention module is mainly composed of two branches (see Fig. 4). The upper branch is used to obtain the mask to generate the attention map for the next adjacent sub-network. The lower branch is the contracting path in next sub-network, $F(x)$ is the feature map after the first residual block. After the convolution operation, the features in the feature map do not change their relative position compared with the original images [5]. So, the two inputs of our attention module are the feature maps from the same scale in two adjacent subnetworks. In the attention branch, $F'(x)$ is feature map before logit chosen from last sub-network, then we use a sigmoid operation to normalize the mask to range to $[0, 1]$, we use the obtained attention map and feature map $F(x)$ for element-wise production. The operation denoted as follows:

$$F_l(x) = F(x) \times (T(x) + 1) \tag{1}$$

In the initial stage of training, the learning effect of the previous sub-network is relatively poor, if the output of the network is directly added as a kind of attention information to the subsequent sub-network, the training effect of the subsequent sub-network will be seriously affected. So we add one for all elements in the attention map, with $T(x)$ approximating 0, $F_l(x)$ will approximate original features $F(x)$. By doing this, we are able to maximize the effectiveness of the attention mechanism.

The attention mask $F'(x)$ is the feature map before logit operation from the last subnetwork, the reason we apply our attention map to the feature map $F(x)$ after a residual block instead of the original input is that they have the same size and number of channels exactly. In this case we don't need a lot of extra operations, such as the up-sampling or $1 \times 1 \times 1$ convolution, will be more efficient.

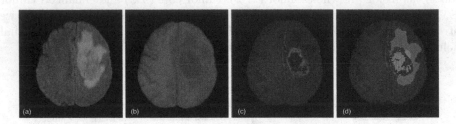

Fig. 5. One slice of brain tumor MRI images in different modalities. (a) T2 Fluid Attenuated Inversion Recovery (FLAIR); (b) native T1-weighted (T1); (c) post-contrast T1-weighted (T1Gd); (d) the ground truth labels that are annotated through expert raters. In the final labels, the whole tumor (green) surrounding the tumor core (red), the enhance tumor (blue) is inside of tumor core. (Color figure online)

3.3   Training

In the training process, we use cross-entropy as the loss function. The formula is as follows:

$$CE(y^i, y^{i'}) = - \sum_{j=1}^{k} 1\{y^i = j\} \log \frac{e^{y_j}}{\sum_{l=1}^{k} e^{y_l}} \tag{2}$$

where y^i is the ground-truth of the ith training sample, $y^{i'}$ means by the model, and k describes the number of classes.

To obtain the global optimal solution of the network, the total loss function of the network is defined as follows:

$$
\begin{aligned}
arg\ min_\theta \mathcal{L} = {}& \alpha \sum_{x_i \in X} \mathcal{L}_{WT}(f_w(x_i), \hat{y}_i^w) \\
& + \beta \sum_{x_i \in X} \mathcal{L}_{TC}(f_t(x_i), \hat{y}_i^t) \\
& + \gamma \sum_{x_i \in X} \mathcal{L}_{ET}(f_e(x_i), \hat{y}_i^e)
\end{aligned}
\tag{3}
$$

In this paper, for the convenience of network design and calculation, we simply set super parameter as follows: $\alpha = \beta = \gamma = 1$.

3.4 Evaluation Metrics

We used the Dice Similarity Coefficient (DSC) and Hausdorff Distance (HD) [13] to evaluate the segmentation accuracy.

The DSC measures a general overlap rate that equally assigns significance to recall rate and false positive rate. For each of the three tumor regions we obtained a binary map with algorithmic prediction $P \in \{0,1\}$ and the ground truth $T \in \{0,1\}$, DSC, sensitivity and specificity are denoted as follows:

$$Dice(P,T) = \frac{|P_1 \wedge T_1|}{(|P_1| + |T_1|)/2} \tag{4}$$

where $\wedge$ is the logical AND operator, P_1 and T_1 represent the set of voxels where $P = 1$ respectively.

Dice score measures the voxel-wise overlap of the segmented regions. A different class of scores evaluates the distance between segmentation boundaries. The Hausdorff distance measures the least squares of all surface points on a given volume to another volume surface. The formulation denotes as:

$$Haus(P,T) = \max \left\{ \sup_{p \in \partial P_1} \inf_{t \in \partial T_1} d(p,t), \sup_{t \in \partial T_1} \inf_{p \in \partial P_1} d(t,p) \right\} \tag{5}$$

Where P_1 is the predict volume and ∂P_1 means its surface, T_1 is the label volume and ∂T_1 represents the corresponding surface, p and t are the surface points of predict volume and label volume, $d(p,t)$ means the shortest least-squares distance from volume P_1 to T_1.

4 Experiments and Results

Table 1. Comparison of the single models we proposed and the models after fusion with other advanced methods on the BraTS'2017 validation set. Since we can only find Dice scores in other methods, we only compare them on the dice score.

Method		Dice		
		ET	WT	TC
Single model	Deepmedic [11]	0.6900	0.8600	0.6800
	Res-U-net [8]	0.732	0.8960	0.797
	Cascaded network [18]	0.7411	0.8896	0.8255
	NMA-Net (axial)	0.7848	0.8945	0.8241
	NMA-Net (sagittal)	0.7681	**0.8966**	**0.8294**
	NMA-Net (coronal)	**0.8006**	0.8958	0.8233
Ensemble model	FCNNs+3D CRF [21]	0.754	0.887	0.794
	Multiple model ensemble [10]	0.738	0.901	0.797
	Cascaded network with fusion [18]	0.7859	**0.9050**	0.8378
	NMA-Net with fusion (ours)	**0.7907**	0.9003	**0.8414**

4.1 Dataset and Pre-processing

The brain tumor MRI dataset used in our experiment are provided by MICCAI BraTS'17 Challenge [13]. The training dataset consists of 285 cases, among them, 75 cases were low-grade gliomas (LGG), which were generally benign tumors with good prognosis; 210 cases were high-grade gliomas (HGG), which were mostly malignant and had very strong diffusivity. The BraTS'17 validation set contains 46 cases with unknown grade. All MRI images are co-registered to the same anatomical template, interpolated to the same resolution ($1\,mm^3$) and skull-stripped.

Each patient's MRI image contains four different sequences, native T1-weighted (T1), post-contrast T1-weighted (T1Gd), T2-weighted (T2), and T2 Fluid Attenuated Inversion Recovery (FLAIR). Different sequences have different imaging characteristics for different tumor regions, and can complement each other in the segmentation task.

Whole tumor (WT) describes an intact part of the tumor, including TC and peri-tumoral edema (ED), which typically shows high intensity signals in the FLAIR sequence. The tumor core (TC) describes the majority of the tumor, which is the tumor that is usually resected. TC includes ET, as well as necrosis (filled with liquid) and non-reinforced (solid) parts of the tumor. ET is a region that exhibits ultra-high intensity in T1Gd, and the presence of necrotic (NCR) and non-enhanced (NET) tumor cores is generally low-intensity in T1-Gd compared to T1 (see Fig. 5). Taking into account the imaging characteristics of these sequences, we selected three more important sequences FLAIR, T1, T1-Gd from the four sequences in the training set as our training data.

Data Pre-processing: In order to alleviate the problem of category imbalance in medical images, we first include the minimum boundary of the pixel and crop the image according to the obtained bounding box. When randomly sampling training patches, we also limit the number of voxels in each category in a patch to ensure that it is higher than a certain number, thus improving the efficiency of the training process.

In the training phase, after cutting out most of the background with zero pixel values, we randomly crop the fixed-size image blocks for training. In order to alleviate the class imbalance, and to avoid a class completely disappearing in one batch data, we need to filter out some image blocks, and only kept those who have a certain number of voxels for all classes. When testing, we perform overlapping sampling, the sampling step is half of the length of the image block, we average the prediction results of the overlapping part, which can improve the prediction accuracy of the edge part of the image block.

To compensate the intensity inhomogeneity in MR images, we first apply the N4ITK based bias correction algorithm to all three scans [16]. Since the MRI intensity varies between different machines and arbitrary units, it is necessary to normalize the intensity of each volume image of all patients. By subtracting the average and dividing by the standard deviation, each MR volume will have zero mean and unit variance.

4.2 Implementation Details

Environment Configuration: In our experiments, the network has been implemented using the TensorFlow framework and training is done on NVIDIA GTX 1080Ti GPU. All the models used Adam optimizer with a learning rate 0.0001 for training. We used cross-entropy as the loss function for all three sub-networks and L2 for regularization, so the total loss is the linear sum of these four losses. The training patch size was $64 \times 64 \times 64$, due to the memory limits of the GPU, we can only set the batch size to 1. In order to prevent the voxel of a certain category from being zero in the patch, and to alleviate the impact of the category imbalance on the model, we set a threshold of 2000 voxels during the sampling process. We trained the model for 200 epochs, which took about 30 h.

3D Residual U-Net Setting: In order to verify the performance of the residual block, we first constructed a basic 3D U-net network, which consists of a contracting (down-sampling) path and an expending (up-sampling) path. The contracting path has 5 convolutional blocks. Every block has two 3D convolutional layers with a filter size of $3 \times 3 \times 3$, stride of 1 in three directions, after the convolution are the batch normalization (BN) and ReLU activation function respectively. For the contracting path, max pooling with stride $2 \times 2 \times 2$ is applied to the end of every blocks except the last block, there is a dropout layer with dropout rate 0.5 after the last block. We use zero padding to maintain the output size of all convolutional layers of the contracted and extended paths. For 3D residual U-net, we only need to replace the basic convolution block with a residual block. Inside each residual block, we repeat batch normalization, ReLU activation function and $3 \times 3 \times 3$ convolution twice.

Table 2. Segmentation results on BraTS'2017 validation set. The input scan numbers 4 means we take FLAIR, T1, T1-Gd, T2 as input, 3 means we only use FLAIR, T1, T1-Gd as input. We submit the results to the official online verification system of BraTS'2017, then we will get the evaluation score for the segmentation results.

Method	Input scan numbers	Dice			Hausdorff Dist.		
		ET	WT	TC	ET	WT	TC
3D U-net	4	0.6849	0.8623	0.6694	5.1036	7.5469	11.8164
3D Residual U-net	4	0.7079	0.8825	0.6737	4.9704	7.0585	11.1943
3D Residual U-net	3	0.7003	0.8800	0.7127	9.6168	8.1839	15.0392

4.3 Results Analysis

In our experiment, we consider a single-view model and a multi-view fusion scenario. Since tumors have different spatial information when viewed from different directions in medical volume images, and we trained the proposed end-to-end multi-attention model with different view image patches extracted from axial, coronal, and sagittal respectively. During testing, we use these three models to

Table 3. Performance of our proposed model on BraTS'2017 validation set. TSS means three separate subnets, and TSAM depicts three subnets with attention mechanism.

Method	Dice			Hausdorff Dist.		
	ET	WT	TC	ET	WT	TC
TSS	0.7402 ± 0.28	0.8748 ± 0.08	0.7658 ± 0.24	5.5044 ± 14.26	9.5330 ± 8.41	8.2216 ± 10.82
TSAM	$\mathbf{0.7848 \pm 0.25}$	$\mathbf{0.8946 \pm 0.07}$	$\mathbf{0.8241 \pm 0.17}$	$\mathbf{2.6783 \pm 2.82}$	$\mathbf{9.4987 \pm 17.04}$	$\mathbf{7.9158 \pm 10.57}$

segment brain images from 3 distinct views and obtain 3 segmentation probability maps. Considering the difference in the effects of learning from different views, we calculated the arithmetic average and weighted averages of the fusion model for making decision. Results on BraTS'2017 validation set are shown in Table 1.

Table 1 shows that the average performance after fusion is better than the single model, which means that the three segmentation results of the fusion multi-view model can eliminate some obvious false positive voxels. These false positive voxels appear only in one of the three results and do not appear in the other two results. We also compared the performance of our proposed model with the top ones of the BraTS'2017 Challenge on the BraTS'2017 validation set. For a single-view model, our proposed end-to-end multi-attention model is able to achieve state-of-the-art performance in segmentation of all tumor subregions. Especially for the enhancing tumor (ET) part, that is, the active part of the tumor which used to determine tumor grade and growth status, our single model can achieve nearly 6% advance of the most advanced single model available on Dice score. The segmentation result on the validation set is shown in Fig. 6.

The proposed **NMA-Net**, which incorporates three different views, also achieved the best Dice score of segmentation in the enhancing tumor and tumor core regions. It's just that the segmentation effect on the whole tumor is a little worse. The main reason may be that there is no addition of attention information for the WT part, and we use fewer sequences than all other methods. As we can see from Table 2, our model is still very competitive with some models that use post-processing methods (3D CRF) and different model ensemble (BraTS'2017 Challenge first place), especially for areas with low voxel ratio and complex boundaries in the image.

4.4 Extensive Discussions

The Effectiveness of Less Input Sequences: We first compare the test performance of using the convolutional block and the residual block on the BraTS'17 validation set. The results are shown in Table 2. From the first two rows of Table 2, it is clear that 3D residual U-net shows a significant improvement in both Dice and Hausdorff distance.

We tried to experiment with fewer MRI sequences for two main reasons. The first reason was to improve training and inference efficiency with less data. The second reason is as we described in Sect. 4.1, as the T2 sequence shows a high signal for both bound and unbound water, the discrimination for the tumor area

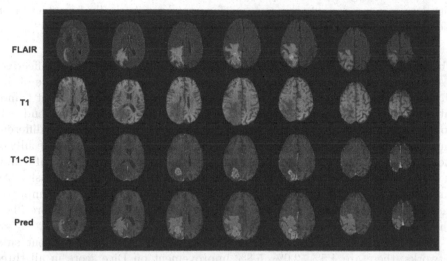

(a) Slices extracted from different depths in the axial plane (Brats17_CBICA_AAM_1)

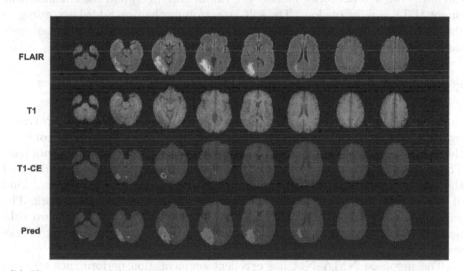

(b) Slices extracted from different depths in the axial plane (Brats17_UAB_3456_1)

Fig. 6. Segmentation results of two different MRI sequences. Both MRI sequences are from the unlabeled validation set. The vertical axis direction from top to bottom is the FLAIR sequence, the T1 sequence, the T1-CE sequence and the corresponding segmentation results of our network, respectively. The horizontal axis represents the slices we extracted along the z-axis of the sequence with 10 voxels step

is not very good, the frequency of utilization of the T2 sequence is relatively low in clinical diagnosis. The experimental results in Table 2 also show that even with less sequences input, the same performance can basically be achieved on Dice score.

The Effectiveness of Attention Mechanism: In order to verify the effectiveness of the attention mechanism, we first removed the attention module of our **NMA-Net** model. We trained three sub-networks to learn the different tumor sub-regions, and kept the same in the parameter setting as the end-to-end network. In the testing phase, we fused the results of the segmentation of different tumor sub-regions from three sub-networks. Compare to segmentation results of the 3D residual U-net which complete segmentation of all sub-regions of tumor at once, we just transform the whole task into multiple different sub-tasks. We can see from the first row of Table 3 that there are 4.0% and 5.3% Dice improvement on the segmentation effects of enhance tumor (ET) and tumor core (TC) which have less voxel and more complex boundaries.

Next, we add the attention mechanism to connect the two adjacent sub-networks, there are 4.5%, 2.0%, 5.8% improvement on Dice score in all three tumor sub-regions. In particular, the improvement of the segmentation results of the latter two sub-networks, namely the tumor core (TC) and the enhancement tumor (ET), is more obvious. The soft attention mechanism added according to the anatomical features of the tumor can make the network learning be more targeted and more focused on learning about areas of interest.

5   Conclusion

In this paper we propose an end-to-end multi-attention model for brain tumor segmentation. By utilizing the anatomical features of the tumor, we decompose the tumor segmentation task with multiple sub-regions into multiple subtasks. The attention mechanism is used to connect the adjacent two sub-networks, and the segmentation result of the previous sub-network is superimposed as a kind of soft attention information on the feature map of the latter sub-network. The addition of attentional information makes the learning of the latter two sub-networks more focused on the region of interest. It is worth noting that we use fewer MRI sequences than all state-of-the-art models.

The proposed **NMA-Net** has excellent segmentation performance on both enhancement tumor (ET) and tumor core (TC), which illustrates the effectiveness of our attention mechanism for this hierarchical tumor segmentation task. In future experiments, we will also extend the model to more segmentation tasks for medical images.

References

1. Chen, X., Liew, J.H., Xiong, W., Chui, C.-K., Ong, S.-H.: Focus, segment and erase: an efficient network for multi-label brain tumor segmentation. In: Ferrari, V., Hebert, M., Sminchisescu, C., Weiss, Y. (eds.) ECCV 2018. LNCS, vol. 11217, pp. 674–689. Springer, Cham (2018). https://doi.org/10.1007/978-3-030-01261-8_40
2. Çiçek, Ö., Abdulkadir, A., Lienkamp, S.S., Brox, T., Ronneberger, O.: 3D U-Net: learning dense volumetric segmentation from sparse annotation. In: Ourselin, S., Joskowicz, L., Sabuncu, M.R., Unal, G., Wells, W. (eds.) MICCAI 2016. LNCS, vol. 9901, pp. 424–432. Springer, Cham (2016). https://doi.org/10.1007/978-3-319-46723-8_49
3. Drozdzal, M., Vorontsov, E., Chartrand, G., Kadoury, S., Pal, C.: The importance of skip connections in biomedical image segmentation. In: Carneiro, G., et al. (eds.) LABELS/DLMIA -2016. LNCS, vol. 10008, pp. 179–187. Springer, Cham (2016). https://doi.org/10.1007/978-3-319-46976-8_19
4. Havaei, M., et al.: Brain tumor segmentation with deep neural networks. Med. Image Anal. **35**, 18–31 (2017)
5. He, K., Zhang, X., Ren, S., Sun, J.: Spatial pyramid pooling in deep convolutional networks for visual recognition. IEEE Trans. Pattern Anal. Mach. Intell. **37**(9), 1904–1916 (2015)
6. He, K., Zhang, X., Ren, S., Sun, J.: Deep residual learning for image recognition. In: CVPR 2016, pp. 770–778 (2016)
7. Huang, G., Liu, Z., van der Maaten, L., Weinberger, K.Q.: Densely connected convolutional networks. In: CVPR 2017, pp. 2261–2269 (2017)
8. Isensee, F., Kickingereder, P., Wick, W., Bendszus, M., Maier-Hein, K.H.: Brain tumor segmentation and radiomics survival prediction: contribution to the BRATS 2017 challenge. In: Crimi, A., Bakas, S., Kuijf, H., Menze, B., Reyes, M. (eds.) BrainLes 2017. LNCS, vol. 10670, pp. 287–297. Springer, Cham (2018). https://doi.org/10.1007/978-3-319-75238-9_25
9. Jégou, S., Drozdzal, M., Vázquez, D., Romero, A., Bengio, Y.: The one hundred layers tiramisu: fully convolutional densenets for semantic segmentation. In: CVPR Workshops 2017, pp. 1175–1183 (2017)
10. Kamnitsas, K., et al.: Ensembles of multiple models and architectures for robust brain tumour segmentation. In: Crimi, A., Bakas, S., Kuijf, H., Menze, B., Reyes, M. (eds.) BrainLes 2017. LNCS, vol. 10670, pp. 450–462. Springer, Cham (2018). https://doi.org/10.1007/978-3-319-75238-9_38
11. Kamnitsas, K., et al.: Deepmedic for brain tumor segmentation. In: Crimi, A., Menze, B., Maier, O., Reyes, M., Winzeck, S., Handels, H. (eds.) BrainLes 2016. LNCS, vol. 10154, pp. 138–149. Springer, Cham (2016). https://doi.org/10.1007/978-3-319-55524-9_14
12. Litjens, G.J.S., et al.: A survey on deep learning in medical image analysis. Med. Image Anal. **42**, 60–88 (2017)
13. Menze, B.H., et al.: The multimodal brain tumor image segmentation benchmark (BRATS). IEEE Trans. Med. Imaging **34**(10), 1993–2024 (2015)
14. Ronneberger, O., Fischer, P., Brox, T.: U-Net: convolutional networks for biomedical image segmentation. In: Navab, N., Hornegger, J., Wells, W.M., Frangi, A.F. (eds.) MICCAI 2015. LNCS, vol. 9351, pp. 234–241. Springer, Cham (2015). https://doi.org/10.1007/978-3-319-24574-4_28
15. Tseng, K., Lin, Y., Hsu, W.H., Huang, C.: Joint sequence learning and cross-modality convolution for 3D biomedical segmentation. In: CVPR 2017, pp. 3739–3746 (2017)

16. Tustison, N.J., et al.: N4ITK: improved N3 bias correction. IEEE Trans. Med. Imaging **29**(6), 1310–1320 (2010)
17. Valverde, S., et al.: Improving automated multiple sclerosis lesion segmentation with a cascaded 3D convolutional neural network approach. NeuroImage **155**, 159–168 (2017)
18. Wang, G., Li, W., Ourselin, S., Vercauteren, T.: Automatic brain tumor segmentation using cascaded anisotropic convolutional neural networks. In: Crimi, A., Bakas, S., Kuijf, H., Menze, B., Reyes, M. (eds.) BrainLes 2017. LNCS, vol. 10670, pp. 178–190. Springer, Cham (2018). https://doi.org/10.1007/978-3-319-75238-9_16
19. Yu, L., et al.: Automatic 3D cardiovascular MR segmentation with densely-connected volumetric convnets. In: Descoteaux, M., Maier-Hein, L., Franz, A., Jannin, P., Collins, D.L., Duchesne, S. (eds.) MICCAI 2017. LNCS, vol. 10434, pp. 287–295. Springer, Cham (2017). https://doi.org/10.1007/978-3-319-66185-8_33
20. Yu, L., Yang, X., Chen, H., Qin, J., Heng, P.: Volumetric convnets with mixed residual connections for automated prostate segmentation from 3D MR images. In: Proceedings of AAAI 2017, pp. 66–72 (2017)
21. Zhao, X., Wu, Y., Song, G., Li, Z., Zhang, Y., Fan, Y.: 3D brain tumor segmentation through integrating multiple 2D FCNNs. In: Crimi, A., Bakas, S., Kuijf, H., Menze, B., Reyes, M. (eds.) BrainLes 2017. LNCS, vol. 10670, pp. 191–203. Springer, Cham (2018). https://doi.org/10.1007/978-3-319-75238-9_17

Application Track

ALBERT-Based Chinese Named Entity Recognition

Haifeng Lv[1,2], Yishuang Ning[1,2(✉)], and Ke Ning[1,2]

[1] National Engineering Research Center for Supporting Software of Enterprise Internet Services, Shenzhen, China
ningyishuang@126.com
[2] Kingdee International Software Group Company Limited, Shenzhen, China

Abstract. Chinese named entity recognition (NER) has been an important problem in natural language processing (NLP) field. Most existing methods mainly use traditional deep learning models which cannot fully leverage contextual dependencies that are very important for capturing the relations between words or characters for modeling. To address this problem, various language representation methods such as BERT have been proposed to learn the global context information. Although these methods can achieve good results, the large number of parameters limited the efficiency and application in real-world scenarios. To improve both of the performance and efficiency, this paper proposes an ALBERT-based Chinese NER method which uses ALBERT, a Lite version of BERT, as the pre-trained model to reduce model parameters and to improve the performance through sharing cross-layer parameters. Besides, it uses conditional random field (CRF) to capture the sentence-level correlation information between words or characters to alleviate the tagging inconsistency problems. Experimental results demonstrate that our method outperforms the comparison methods over 4.23–11.17% in terms of relative F1-measure with only 4% of BERT's parameters.

Keywords: Name entity recognition · CRF · BERT · ALBERT

1 Introduction

Named entity recognition (NER) is an important problem in natural language processing (NLP). The task is to identify entities (typically nouns such as time, place, person name and organization name) with specific labels from text sequences [1]. It has a wide range of applications, such as relation extraction, information retrieval, automatic question and answering, and dialogue system. Whether the relationship can be identified accurately plays a significant role in the subsequent processing.

In recent years, many researchers have proposed the deep neural network (DNN) –based NER methods. The main idea of these methods is firstly to extract the implicit features from text sequences using convolutional neural networks (CNNs) or recurrent neural networks (RNNs), and then to obtain the optimal labeling sequences with conditional random fields (CRFs) [2–6]. Compared with traditional machine learning methods

© Springer Nature Switzerland AG 2020
Y. Yang et al. (Eds.): ICCC 2020, LNCS 12408, pp. 79–87, 2020.
https://doi.org/10.1007/978-3-030-59585-2_7

such as hidden Markov models (HMMs) [7] and CRFs [8–10], the accuracy of these methods has been improved greatly. Different from the English NER task, Chinese NER task generally suffers from many problems such as word-level data sparseness, out-of-vocabulary (OOV) and over-fitting since it relies on the quality of word segmentation. Besides, traditional static word vectors cannot deal with the problem of polysemy [11]. To explore new word vector representation methods, [12] proposed the embeddings from language model, (ELMO), which aims to adjust the character or word vector according to the current context to solve the problems above. In 2018, Google proposed a bidirectional encoder representation for Transformers (BERT) [13] which has achieved good performance on 11 NLP tasks such as text classification, dependency analysis, sequence labeling and similarity. Although BERT is widely used and has good performance in various NLP tasks, it still suffers from the problems such as large huge of model parameters and low efficiency. To address these problems, [14] proposed a simplified version of the BERT model, ALBERT, which shares all the parameters of different layers for the downstream tasks by factoring the word embedding matrix. Tested on various tasks such as GLUE, RACE and SQUAD, ALBERT has not only achieved the state-of-the-art (SOTA) performance, but also has fewer parameters than BERT.

In this paper, we propose an ALBERT-based Chinese NER approach which uses the ALBERT pre-trained model to address the problems mentioned above. Specifically, it first uses ALBERT as the pre-trained model to reduce model parameters. By sharing cross-layer parameters, it can improve both of the performance and efficiency. Besides, it also uses CRF to capture the sentence-level correlation information between words or characters to alleviate the tagging inconsistency problems. Experiments on the 1998 People's Daily Corpus published by Peking University demonstrate the effectiveness and efficiency of our proposed method.

2   Related Work

NER has become a hot topic in NLP field. Researchers from both academia and industry have proposed a variety of methods. The existing NER methods can be divided into three categories: the rule-based method, the statistical machine learning (ML)-based method and the deep learning (DL)-based method. The rule-based method usually extracts the corresponding entities by designing various rule templates. The disadvantages of this kind of method are in two folds: 1) it requires a large amount of prior knowledge; 2) the rule templates cannot cover most of the unstructured data which are very universal in real-world scenarios. As for the statistical ML-based method, it still relies on the feature templates to extract features and integrates language models to recognize entities. For example, [7] uses the HMM-based approach to identify the named entities. [8] proposes a CRF-based approach for Chinese personal name recognition. [9] presents an excel sequence tagging approach based on CRF. [10] proposes JERL to jointly model NER and capture the mutual dependency between the two tasks based on CRF. The DL-based method regards NER as a sequence labeling task, which can recognize entities from text sequences by constructing sequence labeling models. For example, [15] adopts a CNN-based model to extract features and then integrates other features for recognizing entities. [16] combines the BLSTM and CRF models, and proposes the BLSTM-CRF model, which achieves the SOTA performance. In recent years, with the improvement of the performance of computers, researchers have proposed the pre-trained methods which use pre-trained word or character vectors such as Word2vec [17] or Glove [18] that are trained by high-performance computers to capture the context features from text sequences. For example, [19] adopts BERT as the pre-trained model and achieves good results in the NER task. However, because it has huge number of parameters, the time efficiency has been influenced greatly.

3   ALBERT Model

The application of the BERT pre-trained model has achieved significant improvement in various downstream tasks. Moreover, increasing model size has further resulted in better performance. However, due to the limitations of GPU or TPU memories, it becomes increasingly more difficult to train the BERT models with bigger size. To address this problem, [14] proposed a simplified version of the BERT model by designing A Lite BERT (ALBERT) architecture that has significantly fewer parameters than a traditional BERT architecture.

ALBERT is a popular unsupervised language representation learning model. It incorporates two parameter reduction techniques to overcome the memory limitation problem. Firstly, ALBERT uses factorized embedding parameterization to separate the size of the hidden layers from the size of vocabulary embedding, making it easier to grow the hidden size without increasing the size of vocabulary embedding. Secondly, ALBERT adopts cross-layer parameter sharing to prevent the parameter growth with the depth of the network. By leveraging these two techniques, ALBERT can reduce the number of parameters significantly without influencing the performance.

4   Approaches

4.1   Motivation

NER is the task of identifying named entities from text sequences and classifying them into predefined categories, such as person, organization, location, or any other classes of interest. Despite being conceptually simple, NER is not an easy task. The category of a named entity is highly dependent on textual semantics and its surrounding context information. To fully leverage the context information, many researches have used language representation algorithms to transfer the learned information of a trained model to downstream NLP tasks, including NER. Recent advances also demonstrate that the leverage of pre-trained language models [20–23] such as BERT has improved the overall performance significantly, and is highly beneficial when labeled data are scarce. Moreover, the use of the Lite version, ALBERT, not only can improve the parameter efficiency, but also helps with generalization. Motivated by this, we propose an ALBERT-based Chinese NER method which uses two parameter reduction techniques to scale the size and parameters of the pre-trained BERT models. Besides, by sharing the cross-layer parameters, it can better leverage the sentence-level global information obtained by the attention layer.

4.2 Architecture of the Proposed Method

Figure 1 depicts the architecture of the proposed ALBERT-based Chinese NER approach. The model architecture is composed of six layers: the input layer, the embedding layer, the ALBERT layer, the attention layer, the softmax layer and the CRF layer.

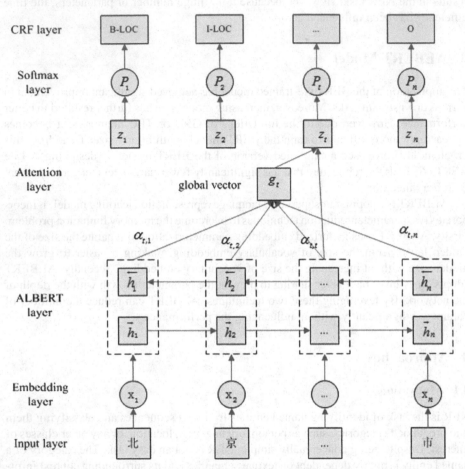

Fig. 1. Architecture of the ALBERT-based Chinese named entity recognition

Firstly, in the input layer, given an input sequence of n tokens $seq = (w_1, w_2, \ldots, w_n)$, it is represented as a sequence vector $X = (x_1, x_2, \ldots, x_n)$ with fixed dimension through the embedding layer. By using the embedding layer, it can capture the semantic relationships among different words or characters. The embeddings are then given as the input to the ALBERT layer to output an encoded token with hidden dimension $H = \left(h_1, \ldots, h_n\right) \in \mathbb{R}^{n \times D}$.

Secondly, to increase the context-sensitive semantic information, a new attention layer on top of the ALBERT layer is used to capture the relation token attention. In the attention layer, we introduce an attention matrix A to calculate the relation between the current target token and all tokens in the sequence. The attention weight value $\alpha_{t,j}$ in the attention matrix is derived by comparing the tth current target token representation x_t with the jth token representation x_j in the sequence:

$$\alpha_{t,j} = \frac{\exp(score(x_t, x_j))}{\sum_k \exp(score(x_t, x_k))} \tag{1}$$

where the score is referred as an alignment function which is represented as follows:

$$score(x_t, x_j) = \mathbf{W}_a (x_t - x_j)^T (x_t - x_j) \tag{2}$$

where $\mathbf{W}_a$ is the weight matrix of the model. For the score of the alignment function, the score value is smaller when the two vectors are more related.

Then a sequence-level global vector g_t is computed as a weighted sum of each ALBERT output h_j:

$$g_t = \sum_{j=1}^{n} \alpha_{t,j} h_j \tag{3}$$

The sequence-level global vector and the ALBERT output of the target token are concatenated as a vector $[g_t; h_j]$ to produce the output of attention layer.

$$z_t = func(\mathbf{W}_g [g_t; h_j]) \tag{4}$$

Thirdly, the softmax layer projects each token's output z_i of the attention layer to the tag space, i.e. $\mathbb{R}^D \mapsto \mathbb{R}^K$, where K is the number of named entity tags. The output scores $P \in \mathbb{R}^{n \times K}$ are computed with a standard softmax function: P = softmax(ZW_p), where $Z = (z_1, \ldots, z_n)$.

Finally, the CRF layer is added to decode the best tag path in all possible tag paths. We consider P as the matrix of scores output by the softmax layer. The element $P_{i,j}$ of the matrix is the score of the jth tag of the ith token in the sequence. We introduce a tagging transition matrix A, where $A_{i,j}$ represents the score of transition from tag i to tag j. The score of the sentence X along with a sequence of predictions $y = (y_1, \ldots, y_n)$ is then given by the sum of transition scores and softmax scores:

$$s(\mathbf{X}, \mathbf{y}) = \sum_{i=0}^{n} A_{y_i, y_{i+1}} + \sum_{i=1}^{n} P_{i, y_i} \tag{5}$$

where y_0 and y_{n+1} are start and end tags, respectively. The model is trained to maximize the log-probability of the correct tag sequence:

$$\log P(y|X) = s(X, y) - \log \left(\sum_{\bar{y} \in Y_X} e^{s(x, \bar{y})} \right) \tag{6}$$

where Y_X is the set of all possible tag sequences. During evaluation, we predict the best tag path that obtains the maximum score given by:

$$\arg \max_{\bar{y}} s(X, \bar{y}) \tag{7}$$

This can be computed using dynamic programming, and the Viterbi decoding [24].

5 Experiments

5.1 Experimental Setup

Data Set. To evaluate the effectiveness of the ALBERT-based Chinese NER model, we used the 1998 People's Daily Corpus published by Peking University. The corpus contains about 30,000 utterances through preprocessing and filtering. In this work, we used about 10,000 utterances for the Chinese NER task. The corpus is split by three subsets which are train:val:test = 8:1:1, with 1000 utterances used as the test set. Each subset contains four kinds of manually annotated named entities: location (LOC), person (PER), organization (ORG) and time (T). We use the "BIO" notation, where "B" represents the starting position of entity, "I" represents the rest position of entity, and "O" represents the word is not an entity. For example, Fig. 2. shows a sample of sentence tagging for Chinese NER.

Fig. 2. A sample of sentence tagging for Chinese NER

Comparison Methods. We compared the performance of the ALBERT-based Chinese NER with some well-known machine learning methods, including CRF, BLSTM, BLSTM with a CRF layer (BLSTM-CRF) and BERT-CRF.

Evaluation Metrics. In all the experiments, we evaluate the NER performance in terms of Precision (P), Recall (R) and F1-measure.

Model Training and Parameter Settings. For our proposed method, we use the pretrained ALBERT model, albert_tiny_zh, to fine-tune the Chinese NER tasks. For fine-tuning, most model hyperparameters are the same as in pre-training, with the exception of the batch size, learning rate, sequence length, and number of training epochs. The dropout probability was always kept at 0.1. The optimal hyperparameter values are task-specific, but we found the following range of possible values to work well across all tasks:

- Batch size: 16, 32
- Learning rate (Adam): 5e−5, 3e−5, 2e−5
- Number of epochs: 3, 4

For the feature-based approach, we use BLSTM with one layer and hidden dimension of d = 100 units for each direction.

5.2 Experimental Results

Table 1 shows the comparison results of our proposed method with other machine learning methods. From the results, we can draw the following conclusions: 1) Using CRF and BLSTM only can achieve good performance (in terms of the three evaluation metrics), indicating the contextual dependencies are important; 2) When BERT is used as the pre-trained model, the performance has improved significantly (4.23–11.17% in terms of relative F1-measure), indicating BERT can better leverage the contextual dependencies to transfer the learned information to downstream tasks; 3) When ALBERT is used as the pre-trained model, the performance has improved slightly, demonstrating the ALBERT model can better leverage the contextual dependencies, sentence-level global information, obtained by the attention layer for modeling.

Table 1. Comparison of Precision, Recall and F1-measure results on the test set (1998 People's Daily Corpus).

Model	Precision	Recall	F1-measure	Parameters
CRF	84.18	85.34	84.76	*
BLSTM	87.96	86.64	87.3	*
BLSTM-CRF	89.78	88.23	89	*
BERT-CRF	93.58	92.94	93.26	108M
ALBERT-CRF	**94.12**	**93.23**	**93.67**	4M

Besides, the improvement in parameter efficiency also shows the most important advantage of ALBERT's design choices, as shown in Table 1: with only around 4% of BERT's parameters, ALBERT achieves significant improvements over BERT, as measured by the difference on test set scores for NER tasks: Precision (+0.54%), Recall (+0.29%), and F1-measure (+0.49%). More interesting observation is the speed of data throughput at training time under the same training configuration. Because of less communication and fewer computations, ALBERT model has higher data throughput compared to the corresponding BERT model.

6   Conclusion

This paper proposes a Chinese ALBERT-based model for Chinese named entity recognition. In this model, the ALBERT model is used as the pre-trained model to transfer the learned context information to downstream tasks. Besides, we also introduce CRF to capture the sentence-level correlation information between words or characters to alleviate the tagging inconsistency problems. Experimental results demonstrate the effectiveness of our proposed method and show superior performance over BERT. Our future work will be committed to using ALBERT-ATTENTION-CRF for NER task.

References

1. Sang, E.F., Meulder, F.: Introduction to the CoNLL-2003 shared task: language-independent named entity recognition. arXiv preprint arXiv:cs/0306050 (2003)
2. Collobert, R., Weston, J., Bottou, L.: Natural language processing almost from scratch, pp. 2493–2573 (2006)
3. Peters, M.E., Ammar, W., et al.: Semi-supervised sequence tagging with bidirectional language models. arXiv preprint, pp. 1756–1765 (2017)
4. Shao, Y., Hardmeier, C., et al.: Character-based Joint Segmentation and POS tagging for Chinese using bidirectional RNN-CRF. arXiv preprint, pp. 173–183 (2017)
5. Rei, M., Crichton, G.K., Pyysalo, S.: Attending to characters in neural sequence labeling models. arXiv preprint, pp. 309–318 (2016)
6. Knobelreiter, P., Reinbacher, C., Shekhovtsov, A.: End-to-end training of hybrid CNN-CRF models for stereo. In: Proceedings of the IEEE Conference on Computer Vision and Pattern Recognition, pp. 2339–2348 (2017)
7. Morwal, S., Jahan, N., Chopra, D.: Named entity recognition using hidden Markov model (HMM). Int. J. Nat. Lang. Comput. (IJNLC) 1(4), 15–23 (2012)
8. Zhao, X.F., Zhao, D., Liu, Y.G.: Automatic recognition of Chinese names and genders using CRF. Microelectron. Comput. 28(10), 122–124+128 (2011)
9. Jiang, W., Wang, X.L., Guan, Y.: Improving sequence tagging using machine-learning techniques. In: Proceedings of 2006 International Conference on Machine Learning and Cybernetics, pp. 2636–2641. IEEE (2006)
10. Luo, G., Huang, X., Lin, C.Y.: Joint entity recognition and disambiguation. In: Proceedings of the 2015 Conference on Empirical Methods in Natural Language Processing, pp. 879–888 (2015)
11. Zhang, Y., Yang, J.: Chinese NER using lattice LSTM, pp. 2227–2237 (2018)
12. Peters, M.E., Neumann, M., Iyyer, M.: Deep contextualized word representations, pp. 1554–1564 (2018)
13. Devlin, J., Chang, M.W., Lee, K.: BERT: pre-training of deep bidirectional transformers for language understanding, pp. 4171–4186 (2018)
14. Lan, Z., Chen, M., Goodman, S., et al.: ALBERT: a lite BERT for self-supervised learning of language representations. arXiv preprint arXiv:1909.11942 (2019)
15. Collobert, R., Weston, J., Bottou, L., et al.: Natural language processing (almost) from scratch. J. Mach. Learn. Res. 12, 2493–2537 (2011)
16. Huang, Z., Xu, W., Yu, K.: Bidirectional LSTM-CRF models for sequence tagging. arXiv preprint arXiv:1508.01991 (2015)
17. Mikolov, T., Chen, K., Corrado, G., et al.: Efficient estimation of word representations in vector space. arXiv preprint arXiv:1301.3781 (2013)
18. Pennington, J., Socher, R., Manning, C.: GloVe: global vectors for word representation. In: Proceedings of the 2014 Conference on Empirical Methods in Natural Language Processing (EMNLP), pp. 1532–1543 (2014)
19. Vaswani, A., Shazeer, N., Parmar, N., et al.: Attention is all you need. In: Advances in Neural Information Processing Systems, pp. 5998–6008 (2017)
20. Yang, Z.L., Dai, Z.H., Yang, Y.M., Carbonell, J., Salakhutdinov, R., Quoc, V.L.: XLNet: generalized autoregressive pre-training for language understanding. arXiv preprint arXiv: 1906.08237 (2019)
21. Liu, Y., Ott, M., Goyal, N., et al.: RoBERTa: a robustly optimized bert pre-training approach. arXiv preprint arXiv:1907.11692 (2019)
22. Lample, G., Ballesteros, M., Subramanian, S., et al.: Neural architectures for named entity recognition. arXiv preprint arXiv:1603.01360 (2016)

23. Sun, S., Cheng, Y., Gan, Z., et al.: Patient knowledge distillation for BERT model compression. arXiv preprint arXiv:1908.09355 (2019)
24. Viterbi, A.J., Wolf, J.K., Zehavi, E., et al.: A pragmatic approach to trellis-coded modulation. IEEE Commun. Mag. 27(7), 11–19 (1989)

Cognitive and Predictive Analytics on Big Open Data

Kevin Hoang, Carson K. Leung$^{(\boxtimes)}$ (iD), Matthew R. Spelchak, Bonnie Tang, Duncan P. Taylor-Quiring, and Nicholas J. Wiebe

University of Manitoba, Winnipeg, MB, Canada
kleung@cs.umanitoba.ca

Abstract. Nowadays, big data are everywhere because huge amounts of valuable data can be easily generated and collected from a wide variety of data sources at a rapid rate. Embedded into these big data are implicit, previously unknown and potentially useful information and valuable knowledge that can be discovered by data science. Due to their value, these big data are often considered as the new oil. In recent years, many governments make their collected big data freely available to their citizens, who could then gain some insights about services available in the city from these open data. In this paper, we present a cognitive and predictive analytic approach to analyze open data for discovering interesting patterns such as tipping patterns. In general, tipping is a voluntary action conceived as social norm that is valuable to service workers in many countries. With the introduction of ride hailing services, traditional taxi services have began facing increased competition. As such, there are increasing interests in factors that are associated with generous tips. Hence, to evaluate the practicality of our approach, we conduct a case study on applying our approach to transportation data (e.g., taxi trip records) from New York City (NYC) to examine and predict tip generosity. Although we conducted the case study on NYC data, our presented approach is expected to be applicable to perform cognitive and predictive analytics on big open data from other cities.

Keywords: Services · Cognitive computing · Big data · Open data · Data science · Data mining · Data analytics · Taxi · Tips

1 Introduction

Big data [3,12,27] are everywhere. Nowadays, huge amounts of valuable data can be easily generated and collected from a wide variety of data sources at a rapid rate. Embedded into these big data are implicit, previously unknown and potentially useful information and valuable knowledge that can be discovered by data science. Due to their value, these big data are often considered as the new oil. Hence, it would be helpful to be able to manage and analyze some of these big data to obtain some interesting results that are relevant to our social

© Springer Nature Switzerland AG 2020
Y. Yang et al. (Eds.): ICCC 2020, LNCS 12408, pp. 88–104, 2020.
https://doi.org/10.1007/978-3-030-59585-2_8

life. *Data science* [4, 7, 16, 18]— which applies data mining [10, 13, 19, 23], machine learning [1] (e.g., deep learning [9], reinforcement learning [31]), statistical and mathematical modelling techniques [14]—to help retrieving information and discovering knowledge from these big data (e.g., biomedical data like genomes [24], financial data [21], social network data [17, 28], transportation data [2]).

In recent years, the concept of *open data* [2, 8] have become more popular. There has been a trend that more and more collections of these big data have been made openly available by scientists, researchers, and non-profit organizations. Moreover, many governments also have made their collected big data freely available to their citizens. Benefits of having these big open data include the following:

- The governments provide an added value of transparency and allow citizens to monitor government activities.
- The governments also provide innovation opportunities to citizens in developing new applications to the open data.
- Citizens could also gain some insights about services available in the city from these open data.

With lots of benefits, many countries have contributed to the idea of *open government* by making government more accessible to everyone. According to the Organisation for Economic Co-operation and Development (OECD)[1], many of its member countries (e.g., South Korea, France, Ireland, Japan, Canada) have put efforts to (a) make their public sector data available and accessible, as well as to (b) support data re-use. In Canada, many cities and provinces have joined the initiative towards providing open data acknowledging the value that is gained in doing so. According to the Canada Open Government Working Group (COGWG)[2], as of May 2020, there were 61 open municipalities, 12 open initiatives, and 12 "open provinces" across Canada in providing open data. Similarly, governments in the USA have also made their data available to citizens. For example, more than 209,000 datasets are available at data.gov, within which 90 datasets are related to taxi services in different cities like Chicago, New York City (NYC), and Seattle.

Taxi services are used around the world as a means of transport from one location to another. In most places, taxis are equipped with a global positioning system (GPS) and a means of wireless communication with a central call server [11]. Some are further equipped with the means to track the status of the vehicle during operation, thus keeping track of attributes such as vehicle location and the timing of various events (e.g., ride start, ride end). The call server is responsible for storing these values recorded by the taxi and its driver, for historical uses, among other reasons. The call server also handles call requests from customers, and dispatches taxis to customers, attempting to maximize the efficiency and reliability of the service.

---

[1] http://www.oecd.org/gov/digital-government/open-government-data.htm.
[2] https://open.canada.ca/en/maps/open-data-canada.

In service industries in many cultures, payment beyond the price of service is voluntarily left for the service workers. The act of providing this additional payment is referred to as *tipping*. Tipping is an interesting phenomenon as it increases the total amount that people end up paying for services. Even though this increased spending is completely voluntary, it still often happens and takes place in many cultures today [20]. To better understand this behavior, Lynn [20] created a guide—namely, a motivational framework for service gratuities and tipping—to categorize the different theories and motives of tipping. Five of the seven categories in his framework are motivations for people to tip:

1. to help employees;
2. to reward service;
3. to gain or keep preferential service;
4. to gain/keep social esteem; and
5. to fulfill a sense of obligation/duty.

The other two categories were reasons to *not* tip:

6. to save money; and
7. to avoid creating or strengthening social status and power difference between the parties involved.

However, the act of giving money voluntarily without any tangible reward seems counter-intuitive as it does not guarantee quality service [25]. This becomes curious when tipping occurs in places that people would never visit again. Is there any relationship between tipping and the quality of services? As an example, only some but not all of the aforementioned motives of service gratuities and tipping were supported by evidence [22]. Additionally, attributes (e.g., person's characteristics, talking to the person by name, being concerned with the person's work conditions) are likely candidates to improve the tipping amount. However, further research is required to support these claims.

Taxi ride is a service that commonly results in tips. Seltzer and Ochs [26] provided a contextual understanding of tipping norms from the perspective of tipped employees. A number of anecdotes from taxi drivers regarding their experiences with tipping were shared. A common thread between these anecdotes is how valuable tips are. Multiple drivers speak of tips being a notable fraction of the total money they make. Additionally, some comment that they do not particularly enjoy driving the taxi, and that it can even be dangerous, but that it is the best way for them to make money.

With this in mind, we aim to identify characteristics of trips that often result in tips that are higher than average. With these insights, drivers may be able to target for trips that are more likely to earn them more generous tips, allowing them to make their job more profitable and financially support themselves and or their families. To do so, we design a cognitive and predictive analytics approach to predict the generosity of tips. To evaluate the practicality of our approach, we conducted a case study in this paper on big open data related to taxi services in a major international metropolitan—specifically, taxi trip records from the NYC[3].

The NYC Taxi and Limousine Commission (TLC)[4], formed in 1971, is an agency of the NYC government responsible for the licenses and regulations of vehicles used for the medallion taxis and for-hire vehicle (FHV) industries in NYC. These vehicles include:

- medallion (yellow) taxis,
- street hail livery (green) taxis,
- FHVs,
- commuter vans, and
- paratransit vehicles.

The dataset we consider in this paper was provided by technology service providers through the Taxicab and Livery Passenger Enhancement Programs (TPEP/LPEP), which were authorized to provide it to the TLC. The TLC provides a large volume of historical taxi ride information as an open dataset. Data in this dataset contains recorded taxi trip event attributes such as

- trip date,
- trip start and end times,
- number of passengers,
- distance travelled,
- approximate pick-up and drop-off locations,
- rate types (e.g., standard, negotiated),
- payment type (e.g., credit card, cash),
- trip cost,
- tip,
- and others.

Collected data spans from year 2009 to year 2019. Probably to preserve the privacy [6,15,30] of passengers, the approximate pick-up and drop-off locations are represented in terms of taxi zones instead of GPS locations.

In this paper, we perform frequent pattern mining and associative classification on a sample of TLC's taxi trip dataset in order uncover common traits of trips that result in generous tipping. *Key contributions of our paper* include the following:

- our design of a cognitive and predictive analytics approach to predict the generosity of tips,
- our evaluation of the approach with a case study on big open data related to taxi services in a major international metropolitan—specifically, taxi trip records from the NYC.

---

[3] https://www1.nyc.gov/site/tlc/about/tlc-trip-record-data.page.
[4] http://www.nyc.gov/tlc.

Our paper provides new insights into notable attributes that affect the generosity of tips provided to taxi drivers. By highlighting these key attributes, we provide taxi drivers with the approach they need to better predict tipping values. In terms of economic impact, having the new knowledge discovered from our approach would help enhance taxi services in order to maximize the amount of money provided to the drivers via tip. By increasing tip values, taxi driver profits would increase, allowing them to better financially support themselves and their families. Although we conducted our case study on the NYC dataset, our approach is expected to be applicable to other cities (e.g., Chicago[5]), provinces/territories or states/federal district (e.g., District of Columbia[6]) and countries (e.g., Canada[7], France[8], UK[9]).

In terms of organization of this paper, the remaining sections are organized as follows:

- The next section (Sect. 2) discusses related work.
- Section 3 presents our big data approach for cognitive and predictive analytics. We explain our key ideas with illustrations on real-life NYC taxi data used for our case study.
- Section 4 analyzes the observations from our case study—an evaluation on cognitive and predictive analytics of tip generosity for NYC taxis.
- Finally, conclusions are drawn in Sect. 5.

2 Related Works

Researchers, especially those interested in knowledge discovery and cloud computing for transportation, have examined taxi trip datasets. Many of them focused on improvement in profit or revenue for taxi drivers. For instance, Tseng et al. [29] analyzed the NYC taxi trip dataset to speculate the profitability of electric taxis. Their study makes use of a Markov decision process in order to determine optimal pick-up locations. Variables for taxi vehicles (e.g., events nearby, time, location), as well as variables specific to electric vehicles (e.g., battery capacity, location of charging stations), are considered. The impacts of these variables are studied and, using the dataset, projected to understand the benefits of up to 1,000 electric taxis in the area. The projection sheds light on the viability of electric taxis, where drivers can earn comparable net revenue, and the carbon emission reductions that would occur. While their study focuses on the benefits of electric vehicles, it does not consider any factors that could correlate to increased profits, but rather compares between current taxi information and projected electric vehicle data.

Among the studies that use taxi trip datasets to improve taxi profit and or revenue, many consider the method of optimizing pick-up locations. For instance,

---

[5] https://data.cityofchicago.org/.
[6] https://opendata.dc.gov/.
[7] https://open.canada.ca/en/open-data.
[8] https://www.data.gouv.fr/en/.
[9] https://data.gov.uk/.

Lee et al. [11] analyzed pick-up patterns for Taxi services in Jeju, South Korea, with this goal in mind. They recommended optimal pick-up locations in order to reduce the frequency that taxis are empty and thus increase the profits of the service. Their analysis makes use of clustering—a technique that involves grouping points in a dataset into "clusters" that share some sort of similarity. In their work, spatial clusters are constructed in order to group pick-up attributes including timestamps, latitudes, longitudes, speeds, directions, and more. This type of grouping is used to accommodate traffic differentiation between different areas and different time frames. Applying the SAS Enterprise Miner (E-Miner) 4.1 to 81,813 pick-up records, pick-up points are grouped for a meaningful, recommendable space entity. The pattern for pick-ups was found to relate to characteristics of each area. Refined clustering and temporal analysis is further used to provide granular recommendations and time-dependent pick-up pattern changes. Their goal of the pick-up pattern analysis is to generate recommended locations for taxis to travel to in order to increase profits. Although it is clear that less downtime can lead to increased profits for taxis, they did not explore how to increase profits with the trips that are already being provided (e.g., by optimizing tips) in the paper. Some factors, such as passenger count, are also excluded from consideration in this paper. We hope to shed light on how taxi drivers can increase profits without necessarily performing more trips.

Noulas et al. [22] investigated the differences in trip prices between Uber (specifically, its basic and cheapest service UberX) and NYC yellow taxis. They found that typically yellow taxis are cheaper than Uber rides. This is because Uber tends to apply surge fees frequently, causing short trips, which are the most common types of taxi or Uber trips, to cost more than the same trip with a taxi would. In contrast to Uber that relies on opaque algorithms to determine the price of rides (which can fluctuate on a minute-by-minute basis with its surge fees), taxi prices are regulated and more transparent. Interestingly, the comparison between the two services included taxi tips reported in the taxi dataset, but only considered Uber's estimated pricing from its application programming interface (API), making it appear that even with tip, taxis in New York are on average cheaper than Uber. Although their article identifies the fact that taxis are making less money even with reported tips, it does not consider the conditions that influence tipping.

Elliott et al. [5] performed analysis on the NYC taxi trip dataset with an intention of discovering patterns regarding tipping. Their study finds that a very large majority of tip percentages are the machine default values of 20%, 25%, and 30%. However, even with the tips of this percentage disregarded, there is no significant correlation between the income levels of pick-up or drop-off location and the tip percentage paid. However, they observed that

- As the income level of the drop-off location decreases, so does the chance that the passenger will provide any tip at all.
- When non-standard tips are provided, it is when the passenger is choosing to tip an amount less than the machine defaults.

With these results in mind, we are interested in analysing the small amount of tips that are both non-default percentages, and higher than the lowest default (and most common) tip percentage of 20%.

3 Our Big Data Analytic Approach

In this section, we first give an overview of our big data analytic approach, and then describe the details on conducting our analytics for cognitive and predictive analytics on big open data.

3.1 An Overview of Our Approach

In general, our big data analytic approach involves the following five key steps:

1. data understanding (e.g., collect relevant data);
2. data sampling (e.g., sample data from collections of relevant big data and focus on the randomly sampled data);
3. data cleaning (e.g., clean the sampled data by fixing or flagging the erroneous, incomplete, and/or inconsistent data);
4. data preprocessing (e.g., preprocess the cleaned data, derived useful fields, transform them into appropriate form for analysis and mining); and
5. data analysis and mining (e.g., mine frequent patterns, form association rules and associative classification rules, make predictions).

These key steps ensure that the data being processed are representatives of the dataset as a whole, and are of high quality, allowing the identified frequent patterns and rules to likely represent relationships in the real world. Among these key steps, the first four steps can be performed once, whereas the last steps—namely, data analysis and mining (e.g., frequent pattern mining, association rule generation, associative classification)—may be executed multiple times depending on the our cognitive parameters (e.g., minimum support threshold for determining if a pattern is frequent).

3.2 Detailed Description of Our Approach

Let us elaborate the aforementioned five key steps when applying our big data analytic approach to big open data of NYC taxi trip records to predict tip generosity of passengers.

Data Understanding. First, let us get a better understanding of the available open big data. In this paper, we examine taxi trip data from NYC. The TLC provides to the public four types of datasets:

1. *Yellow taxi trip records*
   Yellow taxi is one of two main types of taxicabs in the NYC. They are iconic *medallion taxis* painted in yellow, and able to pick up passengers anywhere in the five boroughs—namely, Bronx, Brooklyn, Manhattan, Queens, and Staten Island. The TLC has been receiving yellow taxi trip data from its technology service providers since January 2009, and has made yellow taxi trip records publicly available on its Open Data portal since 2015.
2. *Green taxi trip records*
   Green taxi is another main type of taxicabs in the NYC. They are *street hail livery vehicles*—also known as outer-borough taxis (or boro taxis for short)—painted in apple-green. They are able to pick up passengers in
   - locations above West 110 Street and East 96th Street in Upper Manhattan; and
   - boroughs like Bronx, Brooklyn, Staten Island, as well as Queens but excluding the two airports—LaGuardia Airport and John F. Kennedy (JFK) International Airport,
   so as to improve the availability of taxis in these parts of NYC. As green taxis started operating in August 2013, the TLC has added green taxi trip records from that month onward to its Open Data portal when it made the records as open data in 2015.
3. *For-hire vehicle (FHV) trip records*
   FHVs—which include black cars, community livery cars, commuter vans (also known as "dollar vans"), luxury limousines, private paratransit vehicles, and high-volume FHVs—are usually dispatched by a business base instead of being hailed on the street. The TLC has been receiving FHV trip data from all bases (including app bases) since January 2015, and has made FHV trip records publicly available on its Open Data portal since 2016. Initially in 2015, the records capture the dispatching base license numbers, as well as pick-up dates/times and locations (in terms of taxi zones). Other useful information—such as drop-off dates/times and locations—has been added to the records since 2017.
4. *High volume FHV trip records*
   High-volume FHVs are those FHVs belonging to companies (e.g., Uber, Lyft, Via, Juno) that make more than 10,000 trips per day through their bases. As the TLC created a new license class of high-volume for-hire services (HVFHS) for these high-volume FHVs in February 2019, it has added high volume FHV trip records from that month onward to its Open Data portal.

Once we examined and understood the data, we realized that (a) green taxis pick-up passengers from restricted locations and (b) both FHV trip records (high volume or not) contain limited information (e.g., do not contain fare amount, tip amount, etc.). To avoid distraction, we opted to focus only on *yellow taxi trip records* as they would provide us with the most amount of information for the analytics.

A decade (2009–2019) of yellow taxi trip records are available on the Open Data Portal. Trip records are captured on a monthly basis, for a total of 120 files over the decade. Data on each file are stored in the comma-separated values (CSV) format, making each file of size approximately 600 MB. For instance, the 624 MB file for December 2019 contains 6,896,318 trip records. Each record capture the following fields:

1. vendor ID, which indicates the data provider;
2. pick-up date and time, which are captured by the timestamp when the taxi meter was engaged;
3. drop-off date and time, which are captured by the timestamp when the taxi meter was disengaged;
4. number of passengers, which is entered by the taxi driver;
5. elapsed trip distance (in miles), which is reported by the taxi meter;
6. approximate pick-up location, which are captured by the taxi zone (labelled from 1 and 265 inclusive to cover the five boroughs in the NYC) when the taxi meter was engaged:
7. approximate drop-off location, which are captured by the taxi zone when the taxi meter was disengaged;
8. rate code at the end of the trip, which indicates whether the fares were charged based on:
   - standard metered rate (including trips to and from LaGuardia Airport, as well as trips between JFK airport and NYC destinations outside of Manhattan),
   - trips to and from JFK Airport,
   - trips to Newark Airport,
   - destinations beyond the city limit of NYC such as Westchester and Nassau Counties,
   - negotiated flat fare (negotiated between the taxi driver and passengers), or
   - group ride;
9. a flag, which indicates whether the trip record was stored in vehicle memory or not before sending to the vendor (e.g., when the vehicle did not have a connection to the server, the corresponding trip records are stored and forwarded);
10. payment type, which signify how the passenger paid for the trip: (a) credit card, (b) cash, (c) no charge, (d) dispute, (e) unknown, or (f) voided trip;
11. fare amount, which is calculated by the taxi meter based on time spent and distance travelled for the trip;
12. extra charges, such as
    - rush hour surcharge (e.g., current surcharge is USD 1) incurred during 16:00–20:00 on weekdays excluding holidays, and
    - overnight surcharge (e.g., current surcharge is USD 0.50) incurred during 20:00–06:00 everyday.
13. Metropolitan Transportation Authority (MTA) tax (e.g., current tax is USD 0.50), which is automatically triggered based on the metered rate in use;
14. improvement surcharge (e.g., current surcharge is USD 0.30), which is levied at the flag drop;

15. *tip amount*, which is automatically populated for credit card tips;
16. tolls amount, which sums all the tolls paid in trip (e.g., crossing a toll bridge like the Cross Bay Veterans Memorial Bridge as well as Marine Parkway-Gil Hodges Memorial Bridge; taking a toll tunnel; riding to and from destinations like Westchester and Nassau Counties, as well as Newark Airport); and
17. total amount charged to passengers, which may not include cash tips.

Data Sampling. When handling big data (including big open data), it is not uncommonly to sample data and apply the sampled data for analytics. Then, analysts could verify the findings from the sampled data against the entire dataset. Hence, for the current work, to avoid unintentional bias, we apply random sampling to randomly select records from yellow taxi trip records.

Data Cleaning. Like many other real-life datasets, these yellow taxi trip records also need to be cleaned due to issues like erroneous data, incomplete data, as well as data or schema inconsistency. For instance, over the span of a decade (2009–2019), entries in the datasets may have changed the names of certain fields or the expected values of a field. Moreover, erroneous or irrelevant data may also be present in entries. For example, some trips in the dataset contain non-positive fares and travelled distance. Some trips also have negative tips, while some carry no passengers. Hence, we designed a preprocessor to consolidate all of the legitimate data in our sampled data into a unified structure. In order to address the aforementioned issues, the preprocessor ensures that

– fields across all records are named consistently, and
– their values in the fields are within expected range.

For fields that have changed their names over time, we checked and updated those fields with their latest field names. Consequently, names of all fields would be consistent throughout all taxi trip records. Moreover, when field values are clearly erroneous (e.g., non-positive passenger counts, trip distances, and/or fare amounts; negative tip amounts), we replace the erroneous values by a flag value indicating erroneous data was previously present in this field of this entry.

Data Preprocessing. During the preprocessing step, we derive new fields that can be included in the data analysis and mining step (e.g., association rule formation) later on. These derived fields include:

18. tip percentage, which can be derived from absolute tip amount and total trip amount charged:

$$\text{tip percentage} = \frac{\text{total trip amount charged}}{\text{tip amount}} - 100\% \qquad (1)$$

As Eq. (1) involves division, it may lead to many distinct floating-point number as the resulting tip percentage. To facilitate the later step of analysis and mining, we allow the users to express their preference on the significance or precision of this field. By cognitively incorporating user preference, we round the tip percentage to the nearest integral (say, 5%) increment, nearest integer, 1 decimal place, or 2 decimal places (e.g., tip percentages of 20%, 20.5%, 20.75%). Hence, we derive and capture the resulting *tip percentage range*.

19. day of the week, which can be derived from the pick-up date
20. day of the month, which can be extracted from the pick-up date
21. month, which can be extracted from the pick-up date
22. time period, which can be binned based on the extracted pick-up time:
    - morning (06:00–10:59),
    - mid-day (11:00–15:59),
    - afternoon rush hours (16:00–19:59),
    - early night (20:00–00:59) and
    - late night (01:00–05:59).

These time periods were chosen in order to segment typical weekday work commutes, as well as the periods in between.

With 17 original fields and 5 derived fields, not all $17 + 5 = 22$ fields are needed for analysis and mining. For instance, vendor ID is irrelevant for analysis and mining. Moreover, such keeping all these fields may lead to problems associated with dimensionality curse. Hence, we perform *feature selection* and focus on the following 10 resulting fields that are relevant to our data analysis and mining:

1. pick-up day of the week
2. pick-up day of the month
3. pick-up month
4. pick-up time period
5. number of passengers
6. elapsed trip distance
7. pick-up taxi zone
8. drop-off taxi zone
9. payment type (e.g., credit card, cash)
10. tip percentage range

Data Analysis and Mining. Once the data are cleaned, we divided the cleaned taxi trip records into training and test data. We conducted frequent pattern mining on the training dataset to discover attribute-values that frequently co-occurring together. We then put these frequent patterns in the antecedents or consequents or the rules when forming association rules. To a further extent, we put the tip percentage as consequents of the rules for associative classification. These resulting list of rules are then sorted in descending order of confidence. Associative classification rules in this list help reveal the combinations of attribute-values leading to a certain tip percentage. Moreover, as "a picture is worth a thousand words", we incorporate cognitive mind of users into result explanation. The resulting visual representation help explain for these combinations of attribute-values that lead to the certain tip percentage range.

4 Evaluation

4.1 Results from Frequent Pattern Mining

When paying the taxi fares by credit cards, passengers are usually given three default percentage values for tips. Recall from Sect. 2, a study [5] finds that a very large majority of tip percentages are the machine default values of 20%, 25%, and 30% for NYC taxis. So, a potential user-specific tip percentage ranges would be as follow:

- tip percentage < 20%
- tip percentage = 20% (as a lowest default percentage for credit card machines)
- tip percentage ∈ (20%, 25%)
- tip percentage = 25% (as a medium default percentage for credit card machines)
- tip percentage ∈ (25%, 30%)
- tip percentage = 30% (as a highest default percentage for credit card machines)
- tip percentage > 30%

When applying our cognitive and predictive analytics to open big data of yellow taxi trip records with these percentage ranges, we observed the following frequent patterns about tip generosity:

- To investigate which of the three default tip percentages occurs most frequently, we compared among patterns {tip percentage = 20%}, {tip percentage = 25%} and {tip percentage = 30%}. Among patterns with these three tip percentages, the pattern {tip percentage = 20%} occurs most frequently. This implies that the majority of passengers chose the lowest percentage of 20%.

  To investigate which customer-entered tip percentages occurs most frequently, we ignored patterns {tip percentage = 20%}, {tip percentage = 25%} and {tip percentage = 30%}, and focused on the remainders. Among patterns without the three aforementioned credit card machine default values of 20%, 25%, and 30%, the pattern {tip percentage < 20%} occurs more frequently than other three patterns. Moreover, we also grouped patterns and made the following comparisons:
    - {tip percentage < 20%} with a new "combined" pattern {tip percentage > 20%} (which was formed by combining patterns with tip percentage above 20%)
    - a new "combined" pattern {tip percentage < 25%} with another new "combined" pattern {tip percentage > 25%}
    - a new "combined" pattern {tip percentage < 30%} with the pattern {tip percentage > 30%}

  The comparisons again show that the pattern {tip percentage < 20%} occurs more frequently. This implies that, when the tip amount are entered as a custom value, more passengers entered a percentage below the lowest default percentage (i.e., <20%).

4.2   Results from Association Rule Mining and Associative Classification

In addition to frequent pattern mining, we also conducted association rule mining and associative classification rule mining with the following user-specific tip percentage ranges:

- very low tips, representing tips in the range [0%, 5%)
- low tips, representing tips in the range [5%, 20%)
- usual tips, representing tips that are at 20%
- medium tips, representing tips that are in the range (20%, 50%]
- high tips, representing tips that are above 50%

Then, we observed the following from the resulting rules:

- Rules stating that "pick-up taxi zone = 132 ⇒ tip percentage is medium" and "pick-up taxi zone = 138 ⇒ tip percentage is medium" occur frequently and with high confidence. These rules reveal that, among the passenger picked up from Queens, those who departed from taxi zones 132 (JFK Airport) and 138 (LaGuardia Airport) tended to give medium (i.e., above usual) tips of 20%–50%.
- Among passenger dropped off at Queens, those who headed to taxi zone 138 (LaGuardia Airport) tended to give medium (i.e., above usual) tips.
- Among passenger picked up from Manhattan,
  - those who departed from taxi zones 238 (Upper West Side North) and 263 (Yorkville West) tended to give low tips;
  - those who departed from taxi zones 79 (East Village) and 249 (West Village) tended to give usual tips; but
  - those who departed from taxi zone 230 (Times Sq/Theatre District) tended to give high tips.
- Among passenger dropped off at Manhattan,
  - those who headed to taxi zones 74 (East Harlem North), 75 (East Harlem South) and 186 (Penn Station/Madison Sq West) tended to give very low or no tips;
  - those who headed to taxi zones 236 (Upper East Side North) and 238 (Upper West Side North) tended to give low tips;
  - those who headed to taxi zones 79 (East Village) and 249 (West Village) tended to give usual tips; but
  - those who headed to taxi zone 239 (Upper West Side South) tended to give high tips.

To help visualize the observations from the association rules and associative classification rules, we highlighted the interesting taxi zones on the Taxi Zone Maps (which were made freely available by the NYC TLC) by coloring the corresponding taxi zones based on the five categories of tips: Ranging from very low tips of [0%, 5%) in red, low tips of (5%, 20%) in orange, usual tips of 20% in yellow, medium tips of (20%, 50%] in olive, and high tips of above 50% in green.

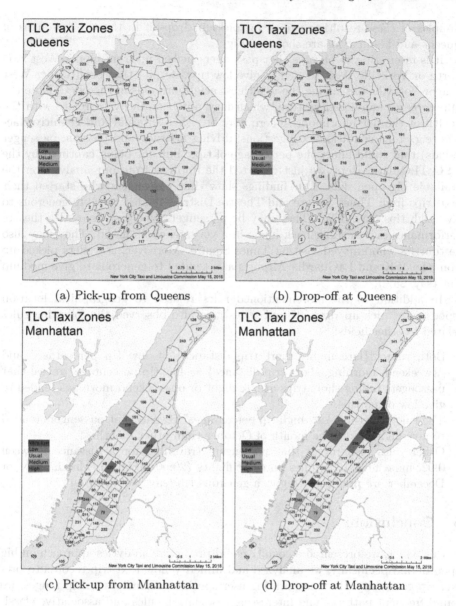

(a) Pick-up from Queens   (b) Drop-off at Queens

(c) Pick-up from Manhattan   (d) Drop-off at Manhattan

Fig. 1. Visualization of analytic results from association rule mining and associative classification (Color figure online)

Samples of these resulting figures for pick-up/drop-off in the two boroughs of Queens and Manhattan are shown in Fig. 1.

It is interesting to observe that passengers picked up from Upper West Side North or Yorkville West tended to give low tips, despite that both Upper West Side or Yorkville are among the wealthiest neighborhoods in the NYC. Note the tipping is an individual gesture, which may not necessarily correlate with the wealth of the neighborhoods. There may be other external and cognitive factors (e.g., road conditions, congestions, driving attitude and passion, passenger moods) that could affect the percentage of tips, but not being captured by the NYC TLC data. Here, we just reported the findings from our analysis on the available big open data. Our findings show that passengers who started their taxi trips from Times Square and Theatre District tended to more generous to give high tips (say, 55%). They may be passengers who just enjoyed a theatre performance and heading back home in a very generous mood. They may also be tourists who enjoyed visiting Times Square. Moreover, travellers picked up from the JFK and LaGuardia Airports also tended to generous to give medium tips (say, 25%).

In addition to the aforementioned rules related to geographical location (specifically, pick-up/drop-off taxi zones), we also observed the following rules related to other fields:

- Both rules "{late night, short trip distance} ⇒ low tip percentage" and "{weekend, morning, short trip distance} ⇒ low tip percentage" reveal that passengers taking short trips at late night or on weekend mornings tended to give low or no tips.
- The rule "{October} ⇒ high tip percentages" reveals that passengers tended to give high tips in the month of October than other months.
- Other rules also reveal that passengers travelling for a distance between 0.025 miles and 0.375 miles on early nights (20:00–00:59) in March, May, or December are predicted to give a generous tip (say, >50% tip).

5   Conclusions

In this paper, we presented a cognitive and predictive analytics approach on big open data. Specifically, we analyzed and mined yellow taxi trip records to predict tip generosity. By incorporating user-specific parameters on tip ranges, we found frequent patterns and interesting association rules and associative classification rules. This discovered knowledge reveal common field attributes associated with high tips. As ongoing and future work, we explore integration of additional datasets (e.g., weather, review/rating of drivers) that could further enhance our analytics on big open data. We also explore transfer learning to apply our learned knowledge from this NYC TLC dataset on yellow taxi trip records to other types of vehicles (e.g., high volume FHV) and/or other cities.

Acknowledgement. This work is partially supported by the Natural Sciences and Engineering Research Council of Canada (NSERC) and the University of Manitoba.

References

1. Ahn, S.: A fuzzy logic based machine learning tool for supporting big data business analytics in complex artificial intelligence environments. In: FUZZ-IEEE 2019, pp. 1259–1264 (2019). https://doi.org/10.1109/FUZZ-IEEE.2019.8858791
2. Audu, A.-R.A., Cuzzocrea, A., Leung, C.K., MacLeod, K.A., Ohin, N.I., Pulgar-Vidal, N.C.: An intelligent predictive analytics system for transportation analytics on open data towards the development of a smart city. In: Barolli, L., Hussain, F.K., Ikeda, M. (eds.) CISIS 2019. AISC, vol. 993, pp. 224–236. Springer, Cham (2020). https://doi.org/10.1007/978-3-030-22354-0_21
3. Dedić, N., Stanier, C.: Towards differentiating business intelligence, big data, data analytics and knowledge discovery. In: Piazolo, F., Geist, V., Brehm, L., Schmidt, R. (eds.) ERP Future 2016. LNBIP, vol. 285, pp. 114–122. Springer, Cham (2017). https://doi.org/10.1007/978-3-319-58801-8_10
4. Dierckens, K.E., Harrison, A.B., Leung, C.K., Pind, A.V.: A data science and engineering solution for fast k-means clustering of big data. In: IEEE TrustCom-BigDataSE-ICESS 2017, pp. 925–932 (2017). https://doi.org/10.1109/Trustcom/BigDataSE/ICESS.2017.332
5. Elliott, D., Tomasini, M., Oliveira, M., Menezes, R.: Tippers and stiffers: an analysis of tipping behavior in taxi trips. In: IEEE Smart-World/SCALCOM/UIC/ATC/CBDCom/IOP/SCI 2017, pp. 880–887 (2017)
6. Eom, C.S., Lee, C.C., Lee, W., Leung, C.K.: Effective privacy preserving data publishing by vectorization. Inf. Sci. **527**, 311–328 (2020)
7. Hayashi, C., Yajima, K., Bock, H.H., Ohsumi, N., Tanaka, Y., Baba, Y. (eds.): Data Science, Classification, and Related Methods. STUDIES CLASS. Springer, Tokyo (1996). https://doi.org/10.1007/978-4-431-65950-1
8. Kassen, M.: A promising phenomenon of open data: a case study of the Chicago open data project. Gov. Inf. Q. **30**(4), 508–513 (2013)
9. Kwon, H., Park, J., Kang, S., Lee, Y.: Imagery signal-based deep learning method for prescreening major depressive disorder. In: Xu, R., Wang, J., Zhang, L.-J. (eds.) ICCC 2019. LNCS, vol. 11518, pp. 180–185. Springer, Cham (2019). https://doi.org/10.1007/978-3-030-23407-2_15
10. Lakshmanan, L.V.S., Leung, C.K., Ng, R.T.: The segment support map: scalable mining of frequent itemsets. ACM SIGKDD Exp. **2**(2), 21–27 (2000)
11. Lee, J., Shin, I., Park, G.: Analysis of the passenger pick-up pattern for taxi location recommendation. In: NCM 2008, pp. 199–204. IEEE (2008). https://doi.org/10.1109/NCM.2008.24
12. Leung, C.K.: Big data analysis and mining. In: Encyclopedia of Information Science and Technology, 4th edn., pp. 338–348 (2018). https://doi.org/10.4018/978-1-5225-2255-3.ch030
13. Leung, C.K.: Frequent itemset mining with constraints. In: Liu, L., Özsu, M.T. (eds.) Encyclopedia of Database Systems, 2nd edn., pp. 1531–1536. Springer, New York (2018). https://doi.org/10.1007/978-1-4614-8265-9_170
14. Leung, C.K.: Mathematical model for propagation of influence in a social network. In: Alhajj, R., Rokne, J. (eds.) Encyclopedia of Social Network Analysis and Mining, 2nd edn., pp. 1261–1269. Springer, New York (2018). https://doi.org/10.1007/978-1-4939-7131-2_110201
15. Leung, C.K., Hoi, C.S.H., Pazdor, A.G.M., Wodi, B.H., Cuzzocrea, A.: Privacy-preserving frequent pattern mining from big uncertain data. In: IEEE BigData 2018, pp. 5101–5110 (2018). https://doi.org/10.1109/BigData.2018.8622260

16. Leung, C.K., Jiang, F.: A data science solution for mining interesting patterns from uncertain big data. In: IEEE BDCloud 2014, pp. 235–242 (2014). https://doi.org/10.1109/BDCloud.2014.136
17. Leung, C.K.-S., Tanbeer, S.K., Cameron, J.J.: Interactive discovery of influential friends from social networks. Soc. Netw. Anal. Min. **4**(1), 154:1–154:13 (2014). https://doi.org/10.1007/s13278-014-0154-z
18. Leung, C.K., Zhang, Y.: An HSV-based visual analytic system for data science on music and beyond. Int. J. Art Cult. Des. Tech. **8**(1), 68–83 (2019)
19. Liu, J., Chang, Z., Leung, C.K., Wong, R.C.W., Xu, Y., Zhao, R.: Efficient mining of extraordinary patterns by pruning and predicting. Exp. Syst. Appl. **125**, 55–68 (2019)
20. Lynn, M.: Service gratuities and tipping: a motivational framework. J. Econ. Psychol. **46**(C), 74–88 (2015)
21. Morris, K.J., Egan, S.D., Linsangan, J.L., Leung, C.K., Cuzzocrea, A., Hoi, C.S.H.: Token-based adaptive time-series prediction by ensembling linear and non-linear estimators: a machine learning approach for predictive analytics on big stock data. In: IEEE ICMLA 2018, pp. 1486–1491 (2018). https://doi.org/10.1109/ICMLA.2018.00242
22. Noulas, A., Salnikov, V., Lambiotte, R., Mascolo, C.: Mining open datasets for transparency in taxi transport in metropolitan environments. EPJ Data Sci. **4**, 23:1–23:19 (2019)
23. Rahman, M.M., Ahmed, C.F., Leung, C.K.: Mining weighted frequent sequences in uncertain databases. Inf. Sci. **479**, 76–100 (2019)
24. Sarumi, O.A., Leung, C.K.: Exploiting anti-monotonic constraints for mining palindromic motifs from big genomic data. In: IEEE BigData 2019, pp. 4864–4873 (2019). https://doi.org/10.1109/BigData47090.2019.9006397
25. Saunders, S.G., Lynn, M.: Why tip? An empirical test of motivations for tipping car guards. J. Econ. Psychol. **31**(1), 106–113 (2010)
26. Seltzer, R., Ochs, H.L.: Gratuity: A Contextual Understanding of Tipping Norms from the Perspective of Tipped Employees. Lexington Books, Lanham (2010)
27. Snijders, C., Matzat, U., Reips, U.: 'Big data': big gaps of knowledge in the field of internet. Int. J. Internet Sci. **7**, 1–5 (2012)
28. Tanbeer, S.K., Leung, C.K., Cameron, J.J.: Interactive mining of strong friends from social networks and its applications in e-commerce. J. Organ. Comput. Electron. Commer. **24**(2–3), 157–173 (2014)
29. Tseng, C., Chau, S., Liu, X.: Improving viability of electric taxis by taxi service strategy optimization: a big data study of New York City. IEEE TITS **20**(3), 817–829 (2019)
30. Wodi, B.H., Leung, C.K., Cuzzocrea, A., Sourav, S.: Fast privacy-preserving keyword search on encrypted outsourced data. In: IEEE BigData 2019, pp. 6266–6275 (2019). https://doi.org/10.1109/BigData47090.2019.9046058
31. Zhang, J., Liu, H.: Reinforcement learning with monte carlo sampling in imperfect information problems. In: Xiao, J., Mao, Z.-H., Suzumura, T., Zhang, L.-J. (eds.) ICCC 2018. LNCS, vol. 10971, pp. 55–67. Springer, Cham (2018). https://doi.org/10.1007/978-3-319-94307-7_5

Short Paper Track

Semantic Enhancement Based Dynamic Construction of Domain Knowledge Graph

Yao Sun[1,3](✉), Lun Meng[2], and Yan Zhang[1,3]

[1] Nanjing Institute of Big Data, Jinling Institute of Technology, Nanjing 211169, China
{suny216,zy}@jit.edu.cn
[2] College of Public Administration, Hohai University, Nanjing 210098, China
m_l_01@163.com
[3] School of Software Engineering, Jinling Institute of Technology, Nanjing 211169, China

Abstract. Knowledge graph (KG) is one of key technologies for intelligently answering questions, which can reduce customer service's costs and improve its self-service capabilities. However, the description of questions is often ambiguous, and the operation and maintenance of online KG based QA services introduces a high cost. To address the above issues, this paper proposes a semantic enhancement based dynamic construction of domain knowledge graph for answering questions. We first employ a model combining LSTM and CRF to identify entities, and then propose a semantic enhancement method based on topic comparison to introduce external knowledge. We employ heuristic rules to get optimal answers, and then periodically update the global KG according to the integer linear programming solver's results. Our approach can achieve a high precise answering results with a low response delay by accurately recognizing entities, automatically mapping domain knowledge to the KG, and online updating the KG. The experimental results show that our approach compared with the traditional method improves the precision, recall and F-measure by 6.41%, 16.46% and 11.17%, respectively.

Keywords: Knowledge graph · Domain feature · LSTM · Semantic enhancement

1 Introduction

As the rapid development of cloud computing and artificial intelligence technologies, intelligent question answering (QA) systems based on knowledge graph (KG) [1] are widely applied in production such as customer services. QA systems establish domain knowledge base by extracting semantics including entities and assertions from the various data, convert the natural language of customers' questions into entities and assertions described in the knowledge graph, and then intelligently answer questions with the optimized algorithm of querying head entities. The intelligent QA systems reduce the effort of manual operations, decrease the fault probability of customer services, provide standard answers to frequent questions, and then guarantee the quality of services. Therefore, a well-designed KG can automatically and intelligently assist customers with low cost.

© Springer Nature Switzerland AG 2020
Y. Yang et al. (Eds.): ICCC 2020, LNCS 12408, pp. 107–114, 2020.
https://doi.org/10.1007/978-3-030-59585-2_9

However, the frequent update of services and various technology stacks have raised great challenges for the construction, maintenance and update of KGs. Current methods often employ lexical and grammatical segmentation, association sequence mining and problem classification templates to construct KGs. However, they are only applicable for determinate training samples in a limited sample space, but cannot deal with the dynamic update of knowledge graphs. Furthermore, existing QA systems often introduce various extra text sources such as web page and documents to expand the knowledge base of entities and assertions. However, an open knowledge base is prone to cause search errors and inaccurate answers because of a large amount of collected data. Thus, we adopt various optimization technologies to construct an enterprise-level KG for customer services, which employ semantic enhancement to dynamically update the KG.

2   Methodology

Figure 1 shows the overall framework of our method including entity recognition, heuristic query and dynamic update. In this section, we will describe them in detail as follows.

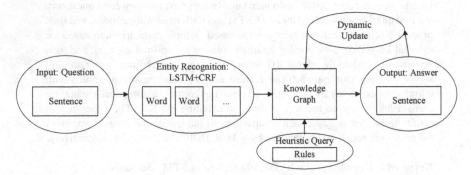

Fig. 1. Method overall framework

2.1   Entity Recognition by Combining LSTM and CRF

To overcome the fuzziness of question description in the QA system, we analyze texts to extract information such as key words and word orders to improve traditional methods of searching header entities and assertions (e.g., semantic analysis, manual labeling). The LSTM model does not consider the constraint between output labels, so we employ a model combining the LSTM and CRF. This model takes the word sequences of a sentence as input, LSTM learns the order information, feeds the probability vector to the CRF layer, and then CRF output predicts best word sequences. We use the formal semantics to describe the LSTM model, where input is a LSTM model M and a question sq_i; output is a predicate p_l and an entity e_h; the enhanced LSTM model is described as $M_{lstm}^i = <p_l, e_h>$.

The output of the trained LSTM model ought to be close to the real value, where the assertion represents users' intention, and the entity represents the domain. To deal with various questions in domain, LSTM mainly uses a dual-phase connected circular network layer (RNN-Layer) and an attention layer (A-Layer) as follows.

Firstly, we segment words, take the question whose length is L as an input, and maps elements into input word vectors $\{x_j\}$ (j = 1, . . . , L). Then, we use the bi-direction LSTM to learn the forward and backward hidden state sequences as follows.

$$f_j = \sigma\left(W_{xf}x_j + W_{hf}h_{0:j+1} + b_f\right)$$

$$i_j = \sigma\left(W_{xi}x_j + W_{hi}h_{j+1:0} + b_i\right)$$

$$o_j = \sigma\left(W_{xo}x_j + W_{ho}h_{j+1:0} + b_o\right)$$

$$c_j = f_jc_{j+1} + i_j \tan h(W_{xc}x_j + W_{hc}h_{j+1:0} + b_c)$$

$$\overleftarrow{h}_j = o_j \tan h(c_j)$$

where f_j, i_j, o_j represent the activation vectors of a forgetting gate, an input gate and an output gate, respectively; c_j is the unit state vector; σ is a sigmoid function; $tanh$ is a double tangent cosine function; o represents Hadamard product.

The model connects forward and backward vectors to obtain $h_j = \left[h_{0:j}; h_{j:0}\right]$, and sets the weight connection layer parameters. The attention weight of the jth word in the word vector $\{x_j\}$ (j = 1, . . . , L) is expressed as α_j calculated as follows.

$$\alpha_j = \frac{exp(q_j)}{\sum_{i=1}^{L} exp(q_i)}$$

$$q_j = tanh(W^T[x_j; h_j] + b_q)$$

Finally, the model forms a hidden state $s_j = \left[x_j; \alpha_jh_j\right]$ with an attention weight α_j, a state sequence h_j and a specific word x_j. Then, we calculate this hidden state s_j to obtain the output $r_j \in R^{d \times 1}$, and the entity/assertion is calculated by the mean value as follows.

$$\frac{\hat{p}_\ell}{\hat{e}_h} = \frac{1}{L} \sum_{j=1}^{L} r_j^T$$

where the weight vector and the bias value are set based on the dataset of training questions and corresponding manually labeled answers, and then two target vectors are calculated with the LSTM model.

2.2 Topic Model Based Semantic Enhancement

To deal with different requirements of various users (e.g., enterprise, family, employee), we select a knowledge base with the greatest tendency, obtain the enhanced texts related to the assertion/entity by comparing the similarity among topics, identify the entity assertion with the LSTM model to construct the global KG. The enhancement method uses external knowledge to online update the knowledge base of KG, thus supporting KG's long-term stable operation and maintenance. The tendency analysis is mainly based on the maximum likelihood estimation and the least square loss estimation on the subject model as follows.

Firstly, as a typical probabilistic method for text analysis, Topic Model (TM) is applicable for two text types. One is graph data used for training KG, and TM adopts the dataset with questions and their corresponding answers to construct the KG. The other is query results, and TM takes the questions processed by the LSTM model as query criteria. The enhanced text is the best matched query result.

We describe the topic distribution with probabilistic hidden semantic analysis [2]. In the dataset of query results with N texts, each text $d_i \in \{d_1, \ldots, d_N\}$ is composed of k unobserved topic variables $z_k \in \{z_1, \ldots, z_K\}$, and each topic variable has different words $w_j \in \{w_1, \ldots, w_M\}$. The joint probability distribution of documents and words (d, w) is as follows.

$$P(d_i, w_j) = P(d_i) \sum_{k=1}^{K} P(w_j|z_k)P(z_k|d_i)$$

where $P(w_j|z_k)$ represents the probability of a word w_j appearing in a topic z_k, $P(z_k|d_i)$ represents the probability of a topic z_k appearing in a document d_i.

The distribution parameters of the hidden topic model can be calculated by the maximum likelihood estimation of the document set as follows.

$$L(D) = \sum_{i=1}^{N \sum_{k=1}^{K} P(w_j|z_k)P(z_k|d_i)} \sum_{j=1}^{M \sum} n(d_i, w_j)lg$$

We use a classical EM algorithm [3] to estimate $L(D)$. However, a PLSA algorithm cannot constraint a document set to some similar topics, and the scale of $P(z_k|d_i)$ linearly grows with the continuous expansion of the knowledge base. TM based methods such as LDA also cannot well describe semantic relationships between documents. Thus, to effectively compare the similarity, we propose a topic similarity calculation method based on PLSA. If an entity in a KG belongs to the topic of a question and its answer, other tail entities connected to it also have a high probability of belonging to the same topic. So, we use the least square loss between a KG and the query result to express the similarity between the entity and the topic as follows.

$$R_v(D_p) = \sum_{i=1}^{|D_p|} \sum_{k=1}^{K} (P(z_k|d_i) - \sum_{e_h \in V} \sum_{e_t \in V} P(z_k|e_h)w(e_h|e_t))^2$$

where $D_p \subset D$ represents the degree that the parts of the query result set match the KG; $w(e_h|e_t)$ represents the weight of the pair of connected entities in the KG, which is calculated as follows.

$$w(e_h|e_t) = -\lg(P(W_{predicate(e_h, e_t)}))$$

where $P\left(W_{predicate(e_h,e_t)}\right)$ represents the probability that two entities are connected with a semantic relationship, and these entities are connected with different paths.

Finally, we can select the tendency result set with maximum likelihood estimation to construct the local KG.

$$L'_{rp} = -(1 - \lambda)L(D_p) + \lambda R_v(D_p)$$

where λ is a bias parameter to balance the topic model and the least squares loss. If $\lambda = 0$, the minimization of L'_{rp} is equivalent to the result set corresponding to the topic with the greatest possibility. If $\lambda = 1$, that is equivalent to the result set that is the closest topic distribution of the entity/assertion in the KG. Thus, we can use the semantic knowledge of external texts and KGs by setting a suitable parameter value.

2.3 Heuristic Querying Rules

To effectively query the global KG by avoiding the non-optimal answers caused by the inefficient graph search algorithm, we employ heuristic query rules to rank candidate set, and select the optimal results from the candidate set as the answers. We consider the question and the global KG to design heuristic query rules as follows.

Historical Candidate Answer Count. By counting historical questions and their answers, we find that questions show relatively aggregated characteristics. The number that a KG query result is selected as a candidate in history, and the richness of the text are two important ranking indexes.

Text Similarity. Answering questions often involves three types of texts, which are the question Q_i, the query results A_j of enhanced semantics, and candidate answers C_k. The optimal answer is often similar to the question and the enhanced semantics. By mapping each word in the texts into the word vector $\{x_j\}$, we calculate the cosine similarity of the candidate answer and the other two types of texts, respectively. Thus, we take the sum of these similarities as a ranking metric.

2.4 Dynamic Update of KG

To guarantee the answer's precision with a lower KG's update cost, the periodic update layer merges external knowledge with the results of integer linear programming (ILP) to support the scale expansion and quality improvement of the global KG. The ILP model quantifies and normalizes users' satisfaction and response time to decide whether the corresponding KG for each question is updated. Thus, the ILP model balances the KG cost and service quality as follows.

We maximize the following objective function:

$$\frac{1}{|KG_L|} \sum_{i=1}^{|KG_L|} uD_i \times uS_i - N \lg \frac{t_{lstm} + t_{augment} + t_{query}}{M},$$

where KG_L represents the collection of local KGs of each question in a period; uD_i represents the update result that is a symbolic function. If the KG is updated, it is set to 1, and otherwise it is set to 0; "$uS_i \subset [0, 100] \cap uS_i \subset Z^+$" represent scores in the training dataset; t_{lstm}, $t_{augment}$, t_{query} represent the processing times in the LSTM model, enhanced semantics and heuristic query, respectively, to measure the cost of operation and maintenance cost; M represents the time reduction factor; N represents the amplification factor adjusted in different configurations.

By setting the above optimization functions and constraints, we can make choices to meet the requirements of maximizing users' satisfaction and minimizing maintenance costs. The actual optimization effect depends on the two scaling factors and the accumulated number of knowledge bases.

3 Evaluation

3.1 Setting

The experiments validate our semantic enhancement method on improving the precision, recall and F-measure of questioning answers, by comparing it with the traditional LSTM based methods of obtaining the head entity/assertion. We adopt a real business dataset of an e-commerce company, which is collect from January to December 2018. The dataset with six hundred assertion labels and eight thousand entity labels includes ten thousand items for training the model, three thousand items for validating the model, and five thousand items for online testing the model. We pre-process and label these data, and then constructs KG to train the model combing LSTM and CRF.

Existing works often employ the precision, recall and F-measure to evaluate methods, but they only count the number of binary problems. We extend the evaluation metrics by defining the matching degree of entities and assertions as follows.

$$precision = \frac{TP}{TP + FP}$$

$$recall = \frac{TP}{TP + FN}$$

$$F1 = \frac{precision \times recall}{precision + recall}$$

where TP (true positive) represents the number of correctly labeled entities and assertions, FP(false positive) represents the number of falsely labeled entities and assertions. We also do a series of experiments to compare our approach with [8] in precision, recall and F1.

3.2 Results

The LSTM activation function employs the loss function PReLU using regularization to constrain the sharing weight parameters, where the penalty value is set as 10^{-6}, the dropout rate of the attention layer is set as 0.15, the weight of the connection layer is set as 0.25, and the bias parameters is set as 0.35. We set these parameters according to our experiences in practice. We query entities and assertions, and select the latest five query results as enhanced semantics. Figure 2 shows that the effects of different bias parameter settings on the precision, recall and F1 of entity assertions on the test dataset. The experimental results show that our semantic enhancement method based on topic modeling and least squares loss can improve the performance metrics in the same dataset. Our method improves the precision by 6.41%, recall by 16.46% and F1 by 11.17%. The experimental results demonstrate that the original topic model cannot fully describe the relevant questions and answers, and the selection of external semantic information can well supplement the single topic model.

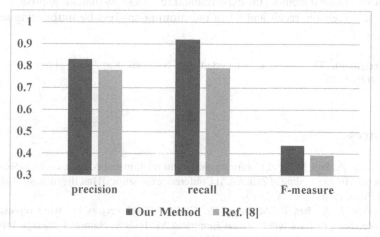

Fig. 2. Result comparison

4   Related Work

Since assertions in natural language have various expressions, KEQA [4] employs LSTM semantic perceptions to discover head entities and assertions, and measures the candidate answer sets with joint distance measurement to deal with ambiguous expressions. CAN [5] constructs a GRU based deep upgrade network for questions, inputs and answers to sense incomplete contextual semantic interactions in interactive systems. Although these methods with limited datasets and static models can improve the precision of querying results in QA systems, they cannot be well applied in industrial scenarios, where business logic frequently changes.

Existing works enhance contextual semantics by introducing external knowledge bases. They enhance entities and assertions to answer questions whose related knowledge is not contained in the KG. FreeBase [6] connects the retrieval results of web pages and KG to enhance semantics. Text2KB [7] takes web search, questions and answers in communities, and common texts as external knowledge bases. DB-pedia [8] proposes a topic model-based information retrieval by introducing multiple knowledge bases. Since external knowledge bases have low reliability, high cost, and unstable performance, these methods cannot achieve well query results in industrial applications.

5 Conclusion

This paper proposes a semantic enhancement based dynamic construction of domain knowledge graph for answering questions. We employ the LSTM-based attention model to overcome the fuzziness of domain questions' expression, use topic comparison based enhanced semantic to construct the local KG, expand the knowledge of the global KG, and then adopt the ILP update strategy to support the dynamic update of KG. Compared with traditional method, the experimental results show that our approach can well improve the precision, recall and F1 of questioning answers by introducing semantic enhancement.

Acknowledgment. This work is supported by National Key R&D Program of China (2018YFB1402900).

References

1. Lin, Y., Liu, Z., Sun, M., et al.: Learning entity and relation embeddings for knowledge graph completion. In: Proceeding of 29th AAAI Conference on Artificial Intelligence, pp. 2181–2187. AAAI Press, Palo Alto, CA (2015)
2. Pennington, J., Socher, R., Manning, C.: Glove: Global vectors for word representation. In: Proceedings of the Conference on Empirical Methods in Natural Language Processing, pp. 1532–1543. ACL, Stroudsburg, PA (2014)
3. Hofmann, T.: Unsupervised learning by probabilistic latent semantic analysis. Mach. Learn. **42**(1), 177–196 (2001)
4. Huang, X., Zhang, J., Li, D., et al.: Knowledge graph embedding based question answering. In: Proceedings of the 25th International Conference on Web Search and Data Mining, pp. 105–113. ACM, New York, NY (2019)
5. Li, H., Min, M.R., Ge, Y., et al.: A context-aware attention network for interactive question answering. In: Proceedings of the 23rd SIGKDD International Conference on Knowledge Discovery and Data Mining, pp. 927–935. ACM, New York, NY (2017)
6. Wang, P., Ji, L., Yan, J., et al.: Learning to extract conditional knowledge for question answering using dialogue. In: Proceedings of the 25th International on Conference on Information and Knowledge Management, pp. 277–286. ACM, New York, NY (2016)
7. Savenkov, D., Agichtein, E.: When a knowledge base is not enough: question answering over knowledge bases with external text data. In: Proceedings of the 39th International SIGIR Conference on Research and Development in Information Retrieval, pp. 235–244. ACM, New York, NY (2016)
8. Sun, H., Ma, H., Yin, W., et al.: Open domain question answering via semantic enrichment. In: Proceedings of the 24th International Conference on World Wide Web, pp. 1045–1055. ACM, New York, NY (2015)

Traffic Incident Detection from Massive Multivariate Time-Series Data

Nicholas Sterling$^{(\boxtimes)}$ and John A. Miller

Department of Computer Science, University of Georgia, Athens, GA, USA
nicksterling@uga.edu, jam@cs.uga.edu

Abstract. Automatic incident detection (AID) aims to programatically detect vehicle traffic incidents from real-time traffic data, and improvements in AID are vital for future technology such as smart-city traffic planning. In this research we use a simple machine learning model (AdaBoost) applied to freely available traffic data from the Caltrans Performance Measurement System (PeMS) to develop a state of the art AID mechanism. In addition we discuss related work in AID to date, introduce and explore the data we use in our experiments, present our methods and results, and discuss conclusions and future work.

Keywords: Traffic flow forecasting · Big data analytics · Automatic incident detection

1 Introduction

Smart-city infrastructure has the potential to improve the lives of anyone who finds themself in an urban environment. One of the areas of greatest potential is in vehicle traffic management. Traffic congestion is not only a nuisance to visitors and residents alike, it is also a major source of lost productivity. While regular traffic congestion during peak use periods is easily predictable, unexpected congestion - often caused by unexpected traffic incidents such as collisions, road hazards, etc. - is by nature unpredictable and requires special attention. Thus, the need for accurate and robust methods of detecting incidents is highly desirable in smart roadway infrastructure.

The most common method of managing traffic incidents involves the use of Automatic Incident Detection (AID) methods, which use data from various sources to identify traffic incidents programatically. One of the most typical data sources used in AID is traffic flow data collected by magnetic Inductive Loop Sensors (ILS), many of which have been installed in dense numbers on freeways throughout the country. ILS detect the number of times (flow) vehicles pass over the magnetic loop and for how long the inductance of the loop changes (occupancy). The data provided by ILS deployed on US roadways has been used for AID since the late 1970s, with research continuing to the present.

The data from sensors is collected into multivariate time-series data. Our work has involved making forecasts based on these data [1]. These forecasts can

© Springer Nature Switzerland AG 2020
Y. Yang et al. (Eds.): ICCC 2020, LNCS 12408, pp. 115–123, 2020.
https://doi.org/10.1007/978-3-030-59585-2_10

be improved by classifying the current state of the road (e.g., at a particular sensor) and using the classifications results in various ways to improve future predictions [2]. Therefore, the problem of time-series classification comes to the forefront. Time-series classification may be for the purpose of classifying time intervals (subsequence of a time-series) or time instances (time points).

The research discussed in this paper provides a novel application of several time-series classification models applied to AID with ILS data, producing a simple and robust AID mechanism which delivers state of the art results. Due to the enormous amount of data collected, only high performance (runtime) classifiers are considered in this study. The fact that these classifiers are to be embedded into a real-time time forecasting system to forecast traffic flow, speed and travel times, only makes the makes the performance requirements more severe. Notably, high quality classifiers such as Support Vector Machines and Neural Networks are not considered due to their computational requirements; while inference from the trained models may be done relatively quickly, nonetheless the need to re-train models on the fly requires that the models evaluated retrain extremely efficiently.

The paper is organized as follows: Sect. 2 provides a summary of AID research to date, Sect. 3 explains the data used in this research, Sect. 4 describes the methods used to apply the modeling techniques to AID, Sect. 5 presents and discusses the results obtained, and Sect. 6 describes conclusions and future work.

2   Related Work

Much of the recent research on AID has focused on using data sources and technologies which are now either newly or at least more widely available. Vehicle-to-vehicle (V2V) and vehicle-to-infrastructure (V2I) communication has become one of the hallmarks of IoT in transportation infrastructure, and both provide data for AID researchers; Popescu et al. researched using V2I data about speed and lane change in [3], and Iqbal, et al. researched both V2I and V2V data in AID in [4].

Regardless of the innovations in traffic sensing technology and data sources, magnetic loop sensor infrastructure remains the most widely deployed sensor technology currently installed on most roads. Thus, research into improving AID results using the classic sensor data is ongoing. Given their popularity and effectiveness, it is unsurprising that Artificial Neural Networks (ANN) and Deep Neural Networks (DNN) are attracting interest in AID research. Recently, Kim in [8] used DNN as a model for AID. This work used a small number of incident (31) and non-incident data (200) with middling results. In 2018 [9] used artificial neural networks (ANN) to expand on the work in [10], which used CCTV data for AID, specifically for detecting incidents in tunnels. Results with accuracy as high as 98% were achieved by Jin et al. using ANN in [11].

Still other recent research has focused on applying various other ML models to traditional magnetic loop sensor data. Rossi et al. studied AID with data from ILS located on freeway off-ramps in [12] using fuzzy logic systems and simulated data. Significantly, Rossi's work did not include analysis on a real-world data set. In [13] Chen et al. use an SVM based approach to detect incidents and achieved high quality results, resuls which nonetheless the current research indicates can be improved on. Li, Chen and Lao in [14] also used SVM in conjunction with an under-sampling technique to correct the imbalanced data, a technique similar to the one presented in this research. The current research achieves results which suggest potential for improvement on all of the above, and confirms those results on real-world data sets.

3   Data

The data used in this study all comes from the California Department of Transportation's (Caltrans) Performance Metric System (PeMS) and is freely available on the web from the PeMS data warehouse (www.pems.dot.ca.gov). All data used in this study was collected between January 1, 2017 and December 31, 2018 in Caltrans's district 4, locations in and around the San Francisco Bay area. Two distinct sets of data are used in this study: district 4 ILS data and traffic incident data reported by the California Highway Patrol (CHP). Please refer to Table 1 for a description of the various fields available in the data sources. The following is a brief description of the two datasets used for this study.

Table 1. A selection of the fields in the various PeMS data sources.

Data source	Field	Description
PeMS Traffic Flow Data	Timestamp	The date and time of the beginning of the summary interval
	Station	The unique station ID for this station
	Flow	Sum of flows over the 5-min period across all lanes
	AvgOcc	Average occupancy across all lanes over the 5-min period
	AvgSpd	Flow-weighted average speed over the 5-min period across all lanes
PeMS Station MetaData	Station	The unique station ID for this station
	Fwy	The freeway this station is detecting on
	Dir	The direction of travel for traffic measured by this station: N, S, E, W
	Postmile	The absolute postmile this station is located at
CHP Incident Data	Timestamp	The date and time of the incident
	Fwy	The freeway this incident occurred on
	Dir	The direction of travel for the freeway this incident occurred on
	Postmile	The absolute postmile this incident occurred at
	Duration	The duration of the incident

3.1   Sensor Data

Among other sources, Caltrans collects traffic data through their PeMS Intelligent Transportation System Vehicle Detector Stations, which includes ILS deployed throughout the California interstate system. The ILS record flow, average occupancy, and average speed data for data flowing past the ILS at 5 min intervals, and the data is available from the PeMS data warehouse at the 5 min resolution. See Table 1 for a selection of the fields available in the historical traffic flow data from PeMS.

In addition to the ILS vehicle traffic data, PeMS also makes available the station metadata for the ILS recording the vehicle traffic data. See Table 1 for a selection of the fields available in the station metadata from PeMS.

3.2   CHP Data

Historical vehicle incident data reported by the CHP computer aided dispatch system is also available through the PeMS data warehouse. Among other information provided by the CHP is the day and time for each incident, the freeway on which the incident occurred and the direction of the freeway, the location of the incident on the freeway in terms of absolute postmile, and the duration of the incident as reported by the responding officer. See Table 1 for a selection of the fields available in the CHP historical data provided by PeMS.

3.3   Relating Sensor Data to CHP Data

At any point in time the flow of traffic over an ILS may be either normal, unobstructed flow or anomalous flow which is obstructed or otherwise affected by some abnormal event, i.e. - a traffic incident; similarly, a sensor reading is either normal or anomalous if the traffic flowing past that sensor is affected by a traffic incident. We now provide our definition of an anomalous ILS measurement. Consider a traffic incident $i = (t_i, fwy_i, dir_i, pm_i, dur_i)$ which occurred at time t_i on direction dir_i of freeway fwy_i at postmile pm_i and which lasted for dur_i many minutes. Next, consider a traffic flow measurement $m = (t_m, s, flow, occ, speed)$ - the $flow$, occ, and $speed$ measurements from time t_m to $t_m + 5$ for some ILS with station ID s. Given s, there is a row in the PeMS station metadata table (s, fwy_s, dir_s, pm_s), giving us both the freeway, fwy_s, and direction, dir_s, the ILS is measuring data on, as well as the absolute postmile of the ILS on the freeway, pm_s, For this research, we define the measurement m as an anomaly if and only if the following conditions are all met:

$$t_i \leq t_m < t_i + dur_i \tag{1}$$
$$fwy_s = fwy_i \tag{2}$$
$$dir_i = dir_s \tag{3}$$
$$0 \leq pm_i - pm_s \leq 1 \text{ for } dir_s \in \{W, S\} \tag{4}$$
$$-1 \leq pm_i - pm_s \leq 0 \text{ for } dir_s \in \{E, N\} \tag{5}$$

In other words where (1) the start of the time interval for m is at or after the beginning of the incident i and before the end of i; (2 and 3) the ILS recording m is located on the same freeway and in the same direction as the incident i; and lastly (4 and 5) the incident occurred within one mile down-stream of the recording station. To understand (4) and (5) remember that the absolute postmiles for a freeway in California begin at 0 from the western terminus of a freeway running East/West and increase by one for each mile travelled eastbound. So, if an incident occurred on the east bound side of a freeway at absolute postmile 10, then the incident is downstream of any sensor which is located on the eastbound side of the same freeway and at an absolute postmile $\leq$ 10, since the postmile increases as you travel eastbound.

Given the above definition, an analogous description of our anomaly detection mechanism is: given the recent history of traffic flow measurements for an ILS sensor we seek to identify whether or not a traffic incident is currently active or has occurred in the past five minutes within one mile downstream of the sensor. While other criteria could be considered as well - for instance, traffic flowing in the *opposite* direction of the freeway on which the incident occurred is often affected by the incident due to the "rubber-necking" of the drivers - this intuitive definition of an anomalous is an appropriate starting place. Using this deterministic definition of an anomalous ILS measurement, we were able to programatically annotate the traffic flow measurements as normal or anomalous with 100% accuracy.

4   Method

The following is a description of the steps taken in the model building process for this study, including a description of the models used, feature engineering, and handling sparse/unbalanced data.

4.1   Models

Several models were trained and evaluated for effectiveness in identifying anomalous traffic measurements in this study, and in all cases the scikit learn implementation was the implementation used unless noted otherwise. The models include: K-Nearest Neighbors (KNN) using 5 nearest neighbors, Naive Bayes (NB), Random Forest (RF) with 100 classifiers Gradient Boosted Trees (GBT) with 100 classifiers and a learning rate of 0.1, ExtraTree classifier with default parameters. and the XGBoost implementation of eXtreme Gradient Boosted trees (XGBoost), In addition, a naïve baseline model was included as well: $c(m_{t,s}) = y_{t-1,s}$, i.e. - classify the measurement from sensor s at time t according to the ground truth for the measurement from sensor s at time $t-1$. Each model (with the exception of the baseline) was trained to classify ILS measurements as either anomalous or normal measurements and evaluated using a moving window training scheme; a window of 28 days worth of data was used to train the model to classify measurements recorded in the next 28 days. For example, an

XGBoost tree model would be trained using all available data from the first four weeks of 2018 - all data from all sensors taken during the first four weeks of January of 2018 - and that model would then be used to identify anomalous measurements taken from any sensor in the second four week window of 2018. In each case, a single model is trained using all available measurements, meaning that the model is sensor-agnostic in that measurements for a new sensor may be incorporated at any time in the training and evaluation process. Results on the effectiveness of the various models are reported in a later section of this study.

4.2 Engineered Features

The ILS data available from the PeMS warehouse contains several informative features: Timestamp, Flow, AvgOcc, and AvgSpd. From these original four features several additional features were engineered to provide additional information for training the models.

Since the data is essentially multi-variate time-series data, seasonal and lag features were engineered to reflect the seasonally correlated and locally consistent nature of the data. Traffic measurements exhibit a weekly periodic nature: traffic measurements taken at 4:00 pm on a Monday are usually very similar to traffic measurements taken at 4:00 pm Monday any other Monday. Deviations from the weekly periodic nature could be indicative of irregular traffic congestion due to incidents. To reflect the weekly periodic nature of the data, four 1-week "seasonal" observation features were added to each data point to reflect the traffic measurements taken one, two, three, and four weeks ago exactly.

In addition to the weekly seasons, traffic conditions typically also exhibit a high degree of local regularity. In other words, traffic measurements taken at any moment in time are likely to be very similar to the most recently recorded measurements, meaning that the most recent previous traffic measurements are likely to be informative about road conditions right now. For instance, if flow measurements have been consistently high over the previous hour and are suddenly very low at the present moment, it may be that the flow is being obstructed by a traffic incident. To illuminate the locally consistent nature of the traffic measurements, 12 five-minute "lag" observation features were added to each data point as well, reflecting one whole hour's worth of previous traffic measurements.

Finally, in addition to the lag and seasonal features of the data, there is inherent information available in the Timestamp feature as well. Traffic patterns are often distinct between days of the week, especially for Mondays, Fridays, and Saturdays & Sundays; the traffic is also periodic throughout the hours of the day, exhibiting rush-hour characteristics at the start of the business day, during the lunch hour and at the end of the business day. The day of the week and the hour of the day when each measurement was taken may be gleaned from the Timestamp feature and included as input to the model as well. Care must be exercised, however, when including categorical features in the ML models: if not handled appropriately, the models may infer a spurious ordinal nature to the features and skew the results. Thus, each category (7 days of the week and 24 h of the day) was included in the training data in one-hot vector encoding.

4.3 Sparse/Unbalanced Data

One of the greatest challenges in anomaly detection is the problem of unbalanced and/or sparse data. Anomalies are by nature rare, and in any training set with normal and anomalous data the normal data will very likely dwarf the anomalous data by comparison. This is most definitely the case in our data, where normal measurements outnumber anomalous measurements by more than 100 to 1. In the face of highly unbalanced data, a ML model for binary classification is likely to be highly biased towards the more representative data, meaning the performance of an ML model for AD will be highly biased towards identifying normal data and perform poorly in identifying anomalies. To combat the problem of unbalanced data we have used the Synthetic Minority Oversampling TEchnique (SMOTE), an up-sampling technique which artificially increases the number of anomalies present in the data. For each sample in the minority class, SMOTE creates synthetic minority samples by randomly perturbing the feature values of one of its k-nearest neighbors. Nogueira et al. developed an open source implementation of the SMOTE algorithm in the imbalanced-learn (imblearn) python package [15], which is compatible with the popular scikit-learn machine learning library for python developers. To generate synthetic samples from a minority sample, we used imblearn's default value of 5 nearest neighbors of the minority sample and default behavior of generating synthetic examples until sample parity is achieved, as these are also the default behavior outlined in the original research presenting the algorithm. Whenever possible, imbleanr's SMOTE implementation was applied to the data in the training window in order to combat the problem of unbalanced data in training the models.

5 Results

We describe the results of the various models in identifying anomalous v. normal ILS measurements in Table 2. The results are reported in terms of precision, recall, and FScore, the harmonic mean between the precision and recall scores. If t_p is the number of true positives identified by the model (anomalies that were classified as anomalies by the model), f_p is the number of false positive identified by the model (normal measurements misclassified as anomalies), and f_n is the number of false negatives identified by the model (anomalies misclassified as normal measurements), then the precision, recall and FScore metrics are calculated as :

$$precision = \frac{t_p}{t_p + f_p}, recall = \frac{t_p}{t_p + f_n}, FScore = \frac{2}{\frac{1}{precision} + \frac{1}{recall}}$$

Achieving an excellent recall is possible through naively categorizing each and every instance as significant, i.e. - anomaly, and achieving an excellent precision score can be "gamed" as well. On the other hand, to achieve a high FScore requires both a robust precision and recall score simultaneously. Thus, the FScore provides a more balanced and informative metric to judge the reliability of a binary classifier.

Table 2. Accuracy metrics for AID models

Model	Rec	Prec	FS	Model	Rec	Prec	FS
Baseline	.888	.888	.888	NB	.818	.038	.073
KNN	.446	.999	.617	RandomForest	.625	.999	.769
ExtraTree	.679	.765	.719	XGB	.952	.999	.975

6 Conclusions and Future Work

From the above results it is clear that the XGBoost tree is a highly accurate model for point classifying the time series measurements for anomaly detection; it was the best performer (as measured by the FScore metric) among all of the predictive models we examined. All other models suffered from either a lack of recall (KNN), lack of precision (RF), or both (ExtraTree, NB) such that their results failed to improve over the naive baseline. Generally speaking, however, the biggest problem for most models was improving on the recall score achieved by the baseline: four out of five models failed to improve on the baseline model's recall score, while just two out of five failed to improve on the precision score, one of which nonetheless achieved a respectable precision score of .765 compared to the baseline precision of .888. These results suggest that future research should focus on improving the precision of AID models over recall.

Secondly, even though the performance of the XGB model in this research is praiseworthy, more research is needed to further verify the validity of those results. To ensure the integrity of the classifiers, the data was trained and evaluated on a rolling window validation scheme with a one month past (training) and future (predicting) window; critically, the models were completely retrained for each window to protect against data leakage into future predictions. Furthermore, while the training samples are augmented with SMOTE upsampling, the testing data is left completely untouched to ensure that the results are not biased towards the SMOTE upsampling. While the middling performance of the majority of the classifiers suggests that the data integrity insurance mechanisms were successful, the near-perfect recall score of our XGB model demands a high degree of scrutiny to verify the integrity of our results.

In addition to the further scrutiny described above, potential areas for future work include the following: collecting more data to improve the validity of the modeling results, investigating the disparity in performance between the various ML models, and integrating the AID module into our future real-time forecasting models which are currently under development. Our preliminary work has shown that traffic flow predictions can be improved by specializing the predictions based on the state of the roadway at the time the classification is made. Our ultimate goal is to use the state of the roadway to improve not just flow predictions but also travel time predictions and route planning recommendations as well.

References

1. Peng, H., Bobade, S.U., Cotterell, M.E., Miller, J.A.: Forecasting traffic flow: short term, long term, and when it rains. In: Chin, F.Y.L., Chen, C.L.P., Khan, L., Lee, K., Zhang, L.-J. (eds.) BIGDATA 2018. LNCS, vol. 10968, pp. 57–71. Springer, Cham (2018). https://doi.org/10.1007/978-3-319-94301-5_5
2. Peng, H., Klepp, N., Toutiaee, M., Arpinar, I.B., Miller, J.A.: Knowledge and situation-aware vehicle traffic forecasting. In: 2019 IEEE International Conference on Big Data (Big Data), pp. 3803–3812. IEEE (2019)
3. Popescu, O., Sha-Mohammad, S., Abdel-Wahab, H., Popescu, D.C., El-Tawab, S.: Automatic incident detection in intelligent transportation systems using aggregation of traffic parameters collected through V2I communications. IEEE Intell. Transp. Syst. Mag. **9**(2), 64–75 (2017)
4. Iqbal, Z., Khan, M.I.: Automatic incident detection in smart city using multiple traffic flow parameters via v2x communication. Int. J. Distrib. Sens. Netw. **14**(11), 1550147718815845 (2018)
5. Karatsoli, M., Margreiter, M., Spangler, M.: Bluetooth-based travel times for automatic incident detection-a systematic description of the characteristics for traffic management purposes. Transp. Res. Procedia **24**, 204–211 (2017)
6. Margreiter, M.: Automatic incident detection based on bluetooth detection in Northern Bavaria. Transp. Res. Procedia **15**, 525–536 (2016)
7. Levy, B., Haddad, J., Dalyot, S.: Automatic incident detection along freeways using spatiotemporal bluetooth data. In: 15th International Conference on Location-Based Services, p. 153 (2019)
8. Kim, D.: Deep learning neural networks for automatic vehicle incident detection. Asia Pac. J. Convergent Res. Interchange **4**(3), 119–128 (2018)
9. Lee, K.B., Shin, H.S., Kim, D.G.: Development of a deep-learning based automatic tracking of moving vehicles and incident detection processes on tunnels. J. Korean Tunn. Undergr. Space Assoc. **20**(6), 1161–1175 (2018)
10. Shin, H.S., Kim, D.G., Yim, M.J., Lee, K.B., Oh, Y.S.: A preliminary study for development of an automatic incident detection system on CCTV in tunnels based on a machine learning algorithm. J. Korean Tunn. Undergr. Space Assoc. **19**(1), 95–107 (2017)
11. Jin, X., Cheu, R.L., Srinivasan, D.: Development and adaptation of constructive probabilistic neural network in freeway incident detection. Transp. Res. Part C Emerg. Technol. **10**(2), 121–147 (2002)
12. Rossi, R., Gastaldi, M., Gecchele, G.: Automatic incident detection on freeway ramp junctions. A fuzzy logic-based system using loop detector data. In: Żak, J., Hadas, Y., Rossi, R. (eds.) EWGT/EURO -2016. AISC, vol. 572, pp. 370–383. Springer, Cham (2018). https://doi.org/10.1007/978-3-319-57105-8_18
13. Chen, L., Xu, P., Ren, T., Chen, Y., Zhou, B., Lv, H.: A SVM-based approach for VANET-based automatic incident detection. Int. J. Simul. Syst. Sci. Technol. **17**(30), 1–5 (2016)
14. Li, M., Chen, S., Lao, Y.: Automatic incident detection algorithm based on under-sampling for imbalanced traffic data. In: Green Building, Environment, Energy and Civil Engineering: Proceedings of the 2016 International Conference on Green Building, Materials and Civil Engineering, GBMCE 2016, Hong Kong, PR China, 26–27 April 2016, p. 145. CRC Press (2016)
15. Lemaître, G., Nogueira, F., Aridas, C.K.: Imbalanced-learn: a Python toolbox to tackle the curse of imbalanced datasets in machine learning. J. Mach. Learn. Res. **18**(17), 1–5 (2017)

Author Index

Printed in the United States
By Bookmasters